941.10857
Campbell
3-23-1995

D0760713

pictures 1-4 are missing

Invisible Country
A journey through Scotland

James Campbell

NEW AMSTERDAM
New York

for Hilary

First published in the United States of America in 1990 by
NEW AMSTERDAM BOOKS
171 Madison Avenue
New York, NY 10016
by arrangement with Weidenfeld & Nicolson, Ltd., London.

Thanks are due to the following authors and publishers for
permission to quote material from:
Selected Poems 1955-1980 by Iain Crichton Smith.
Copyright © 1981, Macdonald Publishers.
Who Owns Scotland by John McEwen.
Copyright © 1977 and 1981. Polygon Books.

Also to the Phoenix Trust for help received while writing the book.

The Library of Congress Cataloging-in-Publication Data is available.

ISBN 0-941533-94-8

This book is printed on acid-free paper.

Printed in the United States of America.

Scotland connotes to the world 'religious' bigotry, a genius for materialism, 'thrift', and, on the social and cultural side, Harry Lauderism and an exaggerated sentimental nationalism, which is obviously a form of compensation for the lack of a realistic nationalism. No race of men protest their love of country so perfervidly as the Scots – no country in its actual conditions justifies any such protestations less. Every recent reference book in any department . . . shows the position to which Scotland has degenerated. *Europa 1926* . . . excludes Scotland completely.

C. M. Grieve (Hugh MacDiarmid),
Albyn or Scotland and the Future, 1927

I have never had to try to get my act across to a non–English-speaking audience, except at the Glasgow Empire.

Arthur Askey

ATLANTIC OCEAN

NORTH SEA

Bettyhill

Rossal

Kinbrace

Badbea
Helmsdale

Portmahomack

Rockfield

Culloden Moor

Inverness

Applecross

Aberdeen

Pitlochry

Alyth

Meigle

Iona Mull Oban

Perth

Dundee

Earraid

Edinburgh

Berwick-upon-Tweed

Glasgow

Selkirk

Kelso

Langholm

0   50 miles

Scotland

Contents

Illustrations

All of the photographs, except Nos 6 and 7, were taken by Fanny Dubes.

Preface

The genesis of this book had much to do with my reading and re-reading of Edwin Muir's *Scottish Journey* (1935), an excellent analysis by an indifferent traveller. Muir drove through Scotland from the Borders to Orkney in the middle of a depression and what he saw reinforced his pessimism about the condition of his native land. He described Scotland as 'a country which is becoming lost to history, gradually being emptied of its population, its spirit, its wealth, industry, art, intellect and innate character'.

What follows here is in no obvious way based on Muir's book, and is certainly not an account 'In the footsteps of . . . ' But I felt that in order to write about any country one had better travel through it and observe and speak to the people who live in it. I would certainly do so if writing about a foreign land; the fact that this happened to be my own country, a tiny part of which I had lived in, ought to make no difference. So, this is not a travelogue or a guide book, nor history or sociology, but is the record of a journey from one end of Scotland to the other, during which I stopped in as many places as was feasible, without setting myself the impossible task of being comprehensive, reporting on encounters with places and people: the Lowlands and the Highlands and the cities; the nationalists, the patriots, the politicians, the intellectuals, the writers and the artists, the landowners, the businessmen, the farmers, the skilled, unskilled, unemployed and unnameable.

I went more or less as my fancy led me, though no doubt there will always be some unconscious motive for choosing one destination before another. Some personal names have been kept and others changed. I owe special thanks to Fanny Dubes for accompanying me on a return journey in order to take the photographs.

Nothing I saw while travelling through a different kind of depression from Muir's fully contradicted the bleak tone of his remarks given above, yet in another way, which this book is part of the effort to understand, everything did; for, fifty years on from his journey, Scotland is no more 'lost to history' than it was then.

Prologue
The Points of a Saltire

Had I been looking for signs, it would have seemed an inauspicious start. I arrived back in Edinburgh on the eve of a national rail strike. Train services to north of the border were already beginning to run down and in London the tube lines were also closed. I was not sorry to be free of the chaos which would follow, and weighed my gratitude against the apprehension which grips me before any kind of travel.

Moreover, I could not help wondering how I was going to move from place to place, as I had turned down the offer of a friend's car. I supposed that until the dispute was settled I would travel by bus and, when that failed, by thumb. Anyway, as I had recently read somewhere, a certain mild fear is an asset to the traveller, prompting him to pay special attention to what is happening around him.

I flew from Heathrow to Edinburgh and during the one-hour flight read an article by a leading member of the Scottish National Party in one of its own journals. It claimed to be seeking a 'quite revolutionary' goal and appealed to the Scots' 'gut patriotism' to achieve the ideal of independence. I soon tired of its oratorical clichés and read the British Airways journal instead. It was Sunday, almost mid-summer, and I had left London warm, but across the 400 miles separating the two capitals the temperature had dropped by ten degrees.

Scotland fears the sabbath and the peripheral city streets were almost deserted. As the airport bus made for the city centre it passed the clock at the west end of Princes Street, still pointing to six twenty-five, as it had done for many years. I welcomed the medley of accents, momentarily strange and deeply familiar, and attempted without success to define what it is that enables me to pick out a Scottish face in a London crowd.

The bus paused at traffic lights before reaching dock. A billboard with its latest poster ripped off revealed fragments of ancient messages; at the foot of the mosaic, I glimpsed two words of a slogan I had no difficulty in deciphering: 'It's Scotland's Oil'. The oil which was discovered in the North Sea was to have provided the means to build a new, independent Scotland. It did not do so, of course, and it seems easy now to say that few really believed that it would. For a time in the seventies, however, something *did* appear to be reawakening in the nation which is proud of being among the first in Europe to find its identity. Whether it is called a renaissance or a rediscovery of national self-consciousness, or just a people's renewed pride in being what they are, it evaporated with the failure of the referendum on devolution in 1979. Afterwards, the same old political struggles emerged in the form of the same endless debates, and the correspondence columns of the *Scotsman* once again became a problem page for sufferers from the Scottish identity crisis. The optimists were devastated and the cynics were satisfied, but Scotland's peculiar stasis simply remained the same.

Yet, although it lost its king and court in 1603, its Parliament in 1707, and even its name in the nineteenth century when it became North Britain, Scotland goes on being Scotland.

Edinburgh guarantees exhilaration in new arrivals. 'The Athens of the North', 'Mine own romantic town', 'The Heavenly City of Philosophers' . . . The catalogue of flattering nicknames is not undeserved. Yet there is another face: 'the sham capital of a sham nation', 'not a centre but a blank'. To ignore the more pitiful aspect of this metropolitan Jekyll and Hyde is to refuse to see Edinburgh and go on living in the kind of nostalgia of which Scotland and the Scots have such great need.

Living in the sham nation exacts a price, and the form which it most commonly takes is the compulsion to regard Scottishness not as a nationality but a destiny – or else to leave.

The Scots are celebrated emigrants from their own country: their diaspora has been the subject of paintings, novels, academic studies, speeches, jokes and even a railway advertisement; and eventually, as I had somehow always expected, I left too.

When I arrived in Edinburgh in the early seventies from Glasgow, and began to form my own opinions about the place, to separate them from the received notions I had inherited along with every other Scot, I experienced something quite new to me, which I can only describe as the feeling of what it is to be Scottish. During my childhood in Glasgow, the predominant feeling among my school-friends was not the force of Scottish patriotism, though that had its place, but loyalist protestantism, which conflicts with it. Although I had always given what vocal and moral support I could muster to Scottish football teams and, when abroad, had spoken up whenever any Scot's integrity was in question, I did so automatically. Whatever pride I felt in being a Scot was a mere reflex of having been born there and not something I could possibly have earned, never having lived outside the country and having been brought up in one of Europe's grimmest industrial cities. But in Edinburgh, which has never fully absorbed the metropolitan influences of industrialism, the past is imperative and sustained exposure to the city's cultural and historical monuments strengthened in me this new feeling of belonging to a distinct tribe with its own myths and traditions. It also fuelled my curiosity as to where this sense of distinctness might lead and what, in the end, it would reveal about the country and about myself.

There need be very little that is romantic about this feeling. Signs of Scotland's past are simply all around you in Edinburgh, in the shape of the castle and Holyrood House, in the pavements of the classical New Town, in the site of the old Parliament and also in the attitudes of the people towards these spectres, attitudes which are deeply reverential in ways quite alien to an inhabitant of the industrial west coast, Glasgow in particular.

Suddenly immersed in this, I began to read Scottish history, in which I was naturally an ignoramus, since Scottish schools teach little of it. How, come to that, can a politically disabled nation create a history for itself? I also began reading Scottish literature, generally regarded as an infrequently flowering branch of English literature. And not least important was the start of my term of office as the editor of the *New Edinburgh Review*, which placed me nearer the centre of Scottish cultural life, forcing me to commission material relevant to the nation's unique problems. One editorial difficulty in particular stood out as the issues of the magazine began to appear. This was the problem of finding good political articles about Scotland which did not rehearse tired old arguments. Clearly, the dearth was not due simply to a lack of writers willing to apply themselves to political subjects; it was the result of a void in Scottish life precisely where politics ought to be.

This void is the most conspicuous thing about modern Scotland – not Edinburgh Castle, nor Holyrood House, nor Loch Lomond. Scotland cannot declare war, cannot grant aid; the people cannot urge their government to act because there is no government. Nobody bothers to ask what Scotland thinks about the arms race, about the Middle East or Central America; nobody bothers because even if there were an answer, it would not relate to the realm of action. The unspoken laws by which Scotland is governed, the assumptions through which the people act, all find their way back to this disconnection.

I am rather fond of the commonplace saying that the primary duty of a writer is to write well; by doing so, he contributes, in however small a way, to the vitality of a literature which helps the nation towards an understanding of itself. This is a difficult enough task, to be sure, but the Scottish writer is confronted with an extra problem since the identity of the nation which prides itself in never having been conquered, can now only be seen by first defining what it is not. It is not, for a start, a part of England, nor even, in reality, of Great Britain, since that beast, like the Loch Ness Monster, doesn't exist except on paper.

In this queer stagnation, prospects for a thriving modern literature are pretty dismal. Writers of fiction in search of a political theme must look either to the past or the future; a great deal of Scottish fiction concerns childhood – the adult writer's personal past. Perhaps the best representative of the Scottish identity, after all, is one of its literature's most celebrated creations – Peter Pan.

In the minds of some, however, the notion of a Scottish identity has never existed. Politics being debarred, conversations with outsiders about Scotland often circulate awkwardly around certain meaningless tokens of Scottishness. At a dinner party in London shortly before I began travelling I found myself seated beside a pleasant young English woman who told me that she had always had a great love of all things Scottish. When she added that she had never in her life set foot in the place, I naturally pressed her to tell me how this infatuation had come about. She supposed that she must have inherited it from her mother, who was 'really Scottish'. Whenever she had had a few drinks, her mother would inevitably start dreaming aloud of her spiritual home. 'You know, the glens and pipers and the lochs – all that sort of thing.'

I could easily imagine – although I tried not to. I also tried, as gently as I could, to explain to my new friend that romantics of this kind, who often spend their Scottish holiday on English-owned estates, were anathema to a Scot: praising haggis and tartan is rather like telling a black American how much you enjoy nigger minstrel shows.

★   ★   ★

I arrived at the house of the friend with whom I would stay while in Edinburgh – the house in which I used to live – to be faced by a broken-down door. But my friend soon appeared to tell me that he himself was responsible, as he had gone out the night before without his key. There were other disasters to report. Heavy rain leaking through the roof had brought the ceiling down in one room recently, and, far worse, an elderly neighbour of whom we both were fond had died in the night.

These catastrophes, minor and major, made me restless and anxious to get away; but I had difficulty getting started. The plans I had laid, and those I attempted to prepare, looked flimsy or impracticable when set against the smallest obstacle. I would leave on Monday – and then it was going to be Tuesday, then Wednesday . . . finally it was Thursday before I got going.

That night I had a dream of being in an aeroplane which bumped along the ground, unable to take off.

I dutifully wrote it down in my journal in the morning, then left by the still unmended door.

★   ★   ★

It was sunny but with a capricious mid-summer chill when I lugged my heavy bag down to Saint Andrew's bus station, where I equipped myself with an armful of newspapers and magazines and bought a pass which allowed me to travel freely on buses throughout the Borders for several days. It was called 'The Waverley Wanderer' and had a picture of Sir Walter Scott printed on it.

I

The Broken Charm

I

Behind the large hotel which occupies one whole side of Kelso's cobbled Market Square, I discovered the Black Bull, a small public house with an oblong, homely bar; pictures crowded all the walls and an overweight barmaid, whom most of the men seemed eager to get close to, served the drinks.

It was Friday night, eight o'clock, the end of another working week, and already the bar was busy. The man standing to my right paid for an extensive round of drinks with a strangely coloured note drawn straight from a brown wage packet. Outside, the evening was light and the air mild. There had been no one in sight when I crossed the wide square, except for a few youths dressed in hideous imitation of hideous city fashions, hanging round a single, spindly motor bike. Once, the driver took off, toured the square, and drew to an abrupt, noisy halt in the place he'd started from. You sensed that that was to be tonight's pastime. For entertainment in Scotland, in city as much as in town, it is difficult to avoid the pub – a form of outdoor life which is careful to remain indoors.

Singles and couples came and went, some staying only for one drink, others anchored already to the bar, where they would remain until closing time. To the right of the door, a totally bald man sat on a two-foot-high stool, playing the accordion. His face had a distant expression as he meandered through an endless medley of reels and folk tunes – all sounding roughly familiar to me but unidentifiable – now and then pausing to take a draught from the pint glass which stood on the floor at his feet, before picking up the thread of the tune again.

I had travelled down by bus in the forenoon, arriving in the small market town just before two o'clock. From Edinburgh, I had first taken the wrong bus and, after three hours, ended up in Berwick-upon-Tweed, where I waited impatiently for an hour or so on the bridge which separates Scotland from England, before embarking on a second journey, shorter this time, along the border itself, through Noreham and Coldstream, to reach Kelso. Hungry and thirsty, I went into the bar of the hotel on the square, a dank place where, to the sights and sounds of a massive television screen, I ate a stale lunch and drank some beer – specially reduced, the barman told me, if drunk in the 'happy hours' between two thirty and five.

The district known as the Borders begins more or less at the Pentland Hills, at the southern fringe of Edinburgh, and comprises, roughly, the area which is marked by Berwick to the east, Biggar to the west and Carter Bar to the south. The heart of the Borders is close to the frontier Scotland shares with England, an area which contains medieval castles and numerous towers in addition to the abbeys at Melrose, Jedburgh, Dryburgh and Kelso.

I chose the Borders as a place to begin simply because it was unknown to me. Travelling around the land of one's birth has some advantages, but among the drawbacks is the fact that the stranger's first glance, at a place or a person, the glance which grants a sudden, unexpected understanding, is not available to the native. He must work hard to achieve such simplicity. The stranger's senses are heightened when he steps out on the street on the first morning, in a place where the air feels fresher, the coffee tastes better, the countenances of the passersby express themselves in unfamiliar facial language. He has a clearer view of the assumptions by which Scotland mutely proceeds from minute to minute than I, who naturally found it difficult to stand back, for I merely stepped behind myself.

Perhaps there was another reason for choosing this starting point. 'Beginnings' in a country, as on a globe, are chosen at random; however, the Borders is the beginning of Scotland, if you define Scotland as starting where England ends. This has some justice, for the Scots are accustomed to being defined – and in many ways define themselves – in opposition to the English.

Geographically, England is a constant presence, as it used to be, and for some still is, a constant threat. This factor has settled deep in the Scottish personality and because of it, and the practice which Borderers have had over the centuries in fending off invaders from across the line, they are often said to be 'more Scottish' than the rest. Every Borders town has its military archive and the map hereabouts is scarred with crossed swords.

I took up a position on a stool at the bar and watched the accordionist. Not once did he acknowledge, smile at or speak to a single soul, even during his intervals for beer. The ample barmaid did not address him as 'love' or 'sweetheart' or 'captain', as she did everyone else. He was too much his own man, and his music, rather than offering part of himself to his listeners, sealed him off from them.

'Does it make you feel like dancin'?'

I turned to see a small man with a precipitous quiff of hair, resting with one arm on a solid black guitar case.

'Cheers.' He drank from his pint glass. 'What brings you here? Just passin' through?'

'For a few days.'

'Holidays?'

'Yes.'

'That's the stuff. Here, though, you're no' a fisherman, are you?'

'No.'

'That's too bad. Willie here's aye lookin' for somebody to take him fishin'. That right, Willie? This boy's on his holidays. What's your name?'

His was Pat.

'And this is Willie. Have a drink. What'll it be? Pint?'

'No, thanks . . . '

'Go on, don't be daft.' He ordered a pint for each of us.

There was a small book of traditional Border ballads on the bar, which I had brought with me to browse through, in case I got bored. As Pat reached forward to pay for the drinks, he noticed it, picked it up and read the spine. Then he stared at me in mock horror.

'Oh, aye – one o' *them*!' He nodded towards the accordionist who was in full swing with a Burns song I couldn't quite put a title to. Pat stamped his foot and shouted loudly, in conflict with the tune:

'*Donald, where's yer troosers!*'

I said, hearing myself sound rather wooden, that it was pleasant to come into a pub and hear live music, an unlikely event in the city. At the comparison between country and city, Willie stepped forward and took my side.

'Used to be you could come in here and half the pub would take a turn.' His lips pursed beneath a thick moustache and he shook his head. 'No now, though.' He stared at the accordionist for a few seconds, but finding his blank face comical, could not suppress a laugh.

'You might be thinkin' he's just a daft auld goat, but he ran off wi' another boy's wife the other day. Aye. Young thing an' a'.'

I looked surprised – I *was* surprised – but before I had a chance to say anything, Willie continued:

'Pat here'll be startin' up on his guitar in a minute or two. There's aye a good barney when Pat gets goin' – everybody joins in until the auld boy canny hear himsel' playin' anymore.'

'What happens then?'

'He packs in and goes home. Have another pint.'

Their openness with strangers may have grown out of their own close friendship, which was bound by separate disasters. Six months before, Pat's wife, a barmaid in the pub, had failed to return home from work at night. Eventually, well after midnight, Pat grew worried and went out to look for her, but when he arrived at the Black Bull it was locked. He went back home and not until next morning did he discover that she had emptied the till and left town with the assistant charge-hand.

'Have they been heard of since?'

He shook his head sadly. 'She'll be back though,' he said, anything but confidently. 'They aye come back. But by that time I'll be set up on my own somewhere, so she can – ' he hesitated – 'look somewhere else if her fancy man's ditched her, which he will have. Take it from me.' Then, in a low voice, as if it was equally painful to speak of, he told me that Willie had come home early from work one day the previous month, to find his wife in bed with another man.

'Only married three months,' Pat whispered, shaking his head in disgust. 'And in his very own bed too.'

'Local?'

He shook his head again. 'Selkirk.'

It was Willie himself who interrupted my mixture of pity and fascination.

'Get your box out now, Pat,' he said. 'Wait till you see the auld boy's face when Pat gets goin'.'

Pat unpacked his guitar and tuned up – it was a twelve-stringer – occasionally palming a chord and staring at me, as if discordancy would register on my face. Finally, he raised the heavy wooden torso chest-high and – with a reluctance which was surprising considering how much they had relished the thought – began to sing. The song was country and western; 'Crying Time'.

The bald man tried to remain oblivious as he continued playing, but it was clear from the animation which came into his face how disconcerted he was. Each musician's eyes strained sideways to read the other's. The accordion groaned on: 'Corn Rigs and Barley Rigs' . . . 'Mairi's Wedding' . . .

'*That it won't be long before it's cryin' time* . . . ' Pat's Borders accent bent the vowels ruthlessly.

Somebody at the back of the pub appealed for a livelier tune – 'Something we can all join in to' – and Pat changed the tempo as much as his repertoire permitted, sometimes beginning a new song before he had reached the end of the one before. They were all country and western numbers. A few minutes earlier, the accordionist had played without a sign that he cared if anyone was listening or not, but now he gripped his instrument purposefully, and though he still stared straight ahead, his face had taken on an obstinate, slightly absurd appearance. Meanwhile, Pat tried to find a tune which everybody knew, one that would lure them from the automatic, noisy conversation to which they had relapsed. No one, except in our immediate circle, was listening at all now. Faithful Willie clapped his hands in time to whatever his friend played.

'Give us "Your Cheatin' Heart", Pat.'

Pat tried 'Your Cheatin' Heart', but conversation in the busy bar did not subside. He gave up with a wave of the hand and returned to the bar and his pint.

'Can't get it goin' tonight,' he said, shaking his head and looking puzzled. 'Don't know what the matter is at all.'

'What's your order, captain?' the barmaid said to me, as I held out a five pound note.

I named everyone's choice and while waiting for her to pour the drinks, noticed that the accordionist had also stopped playing. When I turned my head it was to discover that he had vanished. I was disappointed and felt let down. Pat and Willie were now engrossed in their own conversation, and the bar was filled with the noisy hum of voices. Perhaps the bald man had gone to another place – if so, I wanted to follow him – but on reflection I decided it was more likely he had returned to be with the other man's wife.

II

Distances in the Borders are short, and all the main towns – Selkirk, Galashiels, Hawick and Melrose, in addition to Kelso – could, if so desired, be seen in a single day. You are quite likely to find yourself passing through two or three inadvertently on the way to somewhere else.

I had found a place to stay in Maxwellheugh, a cluster of houses across the long bridge which spans the Tweed, the nearest Kelso has to a suburb, and I decided to keep it as a base for about a week. It was a curious guest house, undergoing a renovation which I sensed had been in process for some time. The proprietor had grand designs – there was already a glass-fronted dining room and some sports facilities – but the overall effect of the current stage was that of a builder's yard, and during the following mornings I ate breakfast and read the newspaper to the sound of joiners hammering nails into planks. The scene was made even more bizarre by the addition of pleasant features such as a duck pond in the centre of the lawn, around which numerous ducklings panicked each time I walked in or out.

The town itself is small enough to meet the people you know by accident once every hour, but the next morning Pat and Willie were nowhere to be seen and Kelso had the atmosphere of a polite Edinburgh suburb. Four streets run from the market square at irregular angles, each parading a row of low, colourful houses. The blight of modern building has been for the most part kept to the outskirts, and the physical outline of Kelso is much the same now as it was a century and a half ago. That applies, by extension, to the whole of the Borders region. Among its burghs are Roxburgh and Berwick, the oldest in Scotland, and the main impression is of a settled land, at peace with the world and itself.

The problems of employing the working members of the hundred thousand inhabitants can no longer be solved on the farms and in the mills, however. Pat and Willie both described themselves to me as mill workers, but one was working as a builder's labourer and the other in a hopeful new electronics factory. A chip is no substitute for a craft, though, and it is without conviction that a Borders man tells you he makes computers.

It might be thought that jobs taken from the farms and mills and placed in factories would change the physical constitution of such an area more drastically than a famine, but not so: the frame remains intact, and the only signs of the surrender of local coherence are the disused railway tracks and stations and hotels, the empty shops and factories and cinemas, the civic buildings deprived of administrative functions, now empty or in use as tourist information bureaux or something else.

Kelso has one small library, to which I went on the morning after my night among the musicians. When I asked for the local history department, the librarian replied that there wasn't one.

'Except these.' He led me past the counter, through a door marked 'Private' and stopped at a shelf containing three books: a handsomely bound two-volume history of the county of Roxburghshire, and a history of Kelso, published in 1825. When I asked to read them the librarian looked worried and said it was forbidden to take them out of the library. I replied that I would look at them here and now. There was another momentary pause and then he lifted up the local history section and with a wag of the head, which meant I was to follow him, walked into the children's library where he positioned me at a table with the books.

James Haig, like most educated people of his time, had no interest in nationalism, which since the failure of the Forty-five Rebellion was tainted not only with the marks of sedition but also with the colours of Popery. His *Topographical and Historical Account of the Town of Kelso* was written at a time when Scotland was often referred to as North Britain (as it was even at the beginning of this century) and is dedicated to 'Her Grace the Duchess of Roxburghe', whose family is still one of the two leading landowners in the Borders. His *Account* is informative (for example, Kelso at the time had three libraries) and pleasantly anecdotal, containing many lists like the following which bring home to the reader the ways in which the economy of the Borders, and therefore the whole manner of living here, has changed in spite of the preservation of surface appearances:

Trade and Manufactures

Kelso, though not entitled to rank among the commercial towns of Scotland, has nevertheless a considerable trade, which affords employment and support to a numerous body of the working classes.

The first and principal branch is the dressing of lamb and sheep skins, the tanning of hides and the currying of leather, all of which are carried on to a vast extent, especially the former – the number of lamb and sheep skins dressed here almost exceeds belief, amounting, on an average, to not less than 100,000.

Pork is here cured to a great extent, which finds a ready sale in the English market.

The manufacture of flannel is pretty extensive, as is also that of different kinds of linen. Woollen cloth is likewise made here, but not in any great quantity, being principally for private use.

The manufacture of hats forms an important branch of the trade of the town; and the quantity of stockings made annually is considerable.

Boot and shoe making is carried on upon a very large scale, supplying not only the town and neighbourhood, but disposing of immense quantities at the different fairs and markets in the north of England.

Candles are also made here, but not in sufficient quantity to supply the consumption of the town and its vicinity.

The shopkeepers, or merchants, in Kelso, are numerous, and deal to a great amount in woollen drapery, haberdashery, hardwares and other household goods. There is also a great demand for the various kinds of grass and other seeds.

Haig also provides brief summaries of the many occasions on which Kelso, like most other Border towns, was taken, burned, laid waste, put under siege or simply invaded by forces from across the border: Edward I took it in 1297; it was burned by Lord Dacres in 1522, burned again twenty years later, and again by Dacres in 1544; in 1570 it was invaded by Elizabeth's army which in the course of a week, 'totally wasted, burned, and destroyed, the vales of Tiviot, Kale, and Bowmont, levelling fifty castles and strongholds and above 300 villages'.

The last time an army was stationed here was in 1745 when Jacobite forces under Prince Charles Edward Stuart, the Young Pretender, assembled for the march into England. (The Old Pretender, James VIII, had been proclaimed king in Kelso's Market Square in 1715.) They took Carlisle and proceeded south as far as Derby, whereupon the increasing threat posed by the Duke of Cumberland made necessary a retreat, which ended in the slaughter at Culloden.

Haig had no time at all, needless to say, for the patriotic adventurism of Bonnie Prince Charlie, yet he ends his account of the rising with a few remarks which, though he would have recoiled from the suggestion, place him implicitly among those who argue that only self-government can bring Scotland properly back to life:

Happily for these kingdoms, the complete frustration of this infatuated attempt, for ever excluded from the thought of the expatriated family the idea of regaining the crown of their ancestors; and since that period the internal peace of the country has remained undisturbed. Of consequence, very little can be supposed to have occurred at Kelso that deserves the notice of the historian . . .

III

To reach the Eildon Hills and Sir Walter Scott's View meant two journeys by bus, of less than half an hour each, preceded by a wait twice as long.

'Beautiful scenery' would pass many tongues after 'Scotland' in an innocent game of word-association, and Scott's View, across the Tweed and the Eildon Hills, distils Borders scenery in the breadth of a single landscape. Enchantingly mountainous, with a serpentine river and lush fields, its proportions are oddly neat; it is both beautiful and 'beautiful'. Particularly appositely for Scott, this area is steeped in legend. It is said that the Eildon Hills, which consist of three compact paps, are the bed of King Arthur and his Knights, who lie sleeping below; also that they were once a single hill but were split into three at the bidding of a thirteenth-century wizard. Then there is the ballad of Thomas the Rhymer which relates how 'True Thomas' spent seven years in one of its valleys with the Fairy Queen and received from her the gift of prophecy. Yet another story concerns Scott himself and explains the modern name which has been given to this landscape. This being his favourite view, he often rode here on his horse, pausing at the point where the harmony of the hills and meadows and the river achieves full splendour, before going on to Abbotsford, the house which he built on the bank of the Tweed in the style of a medieval castle. On the way to Dryburgh Abbey at Scott's funeral, his horse, which was pulling the carriage, is alleged to have paused at the summit, as its master would normally have bid, before going on.

This area of the Borders is often referred to as 'Scott Country'. Passing through, say, Galashiels you might notice the Redgauntlet Restaurant, the Abbotsford Arms, a Waverley Hotel and a Kenilworth Avenue. Similarly, the things for which he is best remembered here – the View, Abbotsford House, his burial place at Dryburgh, the Court House in Selkirk – are chiefly the concern of the tourist trade. No other British writer who is nowadays read so little can have supplied that industry with so much. Scott's contribution has helped to create the prevalent idea that Scotland is a land almost totally occupied by castles, lochs and the skirl of the bagpipes. He was a great genius, but he could not resist the power of his imagination and never hesitated to put it to use in adorning plain reality.

He led a double life, both intellectually and socially. Solidly pro-Union, he could not forsake the romance of Jacobite adventures, and he ensured that no one suspected the pleasant, lame Mr Scott, the Sheriff of Selkirkshire, of being the author of *Waverley*. As Edwin Muir wrote, he took from both his worlds the cheapest they could give him, romantic illusion and worldly advantage.

There are countless corroborations of the paradox of Scott's nature, and in Selkirk I came across another, slightly unusual one.

Adelbert Doisy de Villargenes was wounded and taken prisoner by the British after a skirmish in the Spanish Peninsula while serving in Napoleon's *Grande Armée*. He was shipped to Leith, where he landed on 11 October 1811, and from there was sent, along with 167 other prisoners-of-war, to Selkirk. At first there was some difficulty securing accommodation for the Frenchmen in a town of only two thousand inhabitants. However, their ability and willingness to pay cash soon sorted things out among their comparatively poor hosts. Doisy himself was not especially rich, but some of his fellow prisoners were: one received an annual allowance of £1,000, about twice what his Borders landlord could expect to earn in a lifetime. By the end of hostilities in 1814 it was estimated that the Frenchmen had spent almost £20,000 in two and a half years in a town without its own manufactures.

Given the reasons for their presence, the Frenchmen's integration into the life of Selkirk seems to have worked well, and to some extent they took over its cultural aspect: a musical society was established, a theatre built where performances tragic, comic and vaudeville were staged every Wednesday evening, and a café was made out of the buildings in the Market Place, which, however, admitted only Frenchmen. (It is still a café, though now Scots-Italian.)

The French prisoners were permitted a certain amount of freedom of movement during their stay and they became acquainted with several people in the district: a retired lawyer who alarmed the foreigners with his dispensations of 'super abundant libations'; a gentleman farmer called Anderson, who politely offered them the use of his river for fishing; and another farmer, Mr Thorburn, who introduced them to 'Scotch dishes such as grilled lamb's head, haggis, hotch-potch, and a marvellous cheese of his own making'. There was also a lawyer of repute, with whom a Frenchman called Tarnier grew friendly, the two men sharing an enthusiasm for literature and history. The lawyer, who was also the Sheriff of the shire, often invited Monsieur Tarnier to dine at his house and requested that he bring three of his cultured friends with him each time. Doisy, who after his release returned to France and thence to America where he published a life of Napoleon, visited on several occasions.

It would be, as far as I can remember, about the month of February, 1813, and our mode of procedure was as follows: In the twilight, those who were invited repaired to the boundary . . . there a carriage awaited us, which took us at a good pace to Abbotsford where we were most graciously received by our host.

Our host appeared to us in quite a different aspect to that under which we had known him passing in the streets of Selkirk. There, he gave us the impression of being a cheery, good-natured man whose face was rather ordinary and whose carriage was somewhat common, and halting in his gait, this being probably due to his lameness. At Abbotsford, on the contrary, we found him a gentleman full of cordiality and gaiety, receiving his guests in a fashion as amiable as it was delicate. The rooms were spacious, and well-lighted; the table without being sumptuous, was on the whole, *recherché*. One need not expect me to describe very exactly the surroundings of Abbotsford as on the occasions I was privileged to be there, we arrived in the twilight and we returned when it was quite dark by the same means of locomotion.

But the general theme of our conversation has remained immutably fixed on my memory. The principal subject of our discussions did not turn on politics, but on minute details concerning the French army. All that particularly referred to Napoleon and, above all, traits and anecdotes, appeared to interest our host in the highest degree, who always found the means, we observed, to bring the conversation to this subject if it happened to have diverged in any way. As can be imagined, we took care to repeat nothing unfavourable regarding the character and honour of our beloved Emperor.

We little suspected that our host was gathering material for a work published ten years later under the title 'A Life of Napoleon Bonaparte'. In this work, which is a stain on the character of its otherwise illustrious author, Sir Walter Scott cites events connected with the Emperor, the greater part of which was communicated to him by us, but distorted each incident with malevolent insinuations and self-invented motives of action derogatory to the honour of Napoleon.

Thus passed and ended my brief acquaintance with so illustrious a personage.

Scott's industry on behalf of the Border ballads was his first great literary labour but over the last hundred years or so it has been discredited. In good faith, he attempted to repay the oral tradition for everything it had given him, and with the help of James Hogg he collected 112 songs and published them, with lengthy notes and commentary, under the title, *Minstrelsy of the Scottish Border*. For an idea of how the Borders felt during the period before the Union of the Crowns, when the line between Scotland and England was likely to be shifted from one day to the next, the Border ballads provide the best record. 'Johnie Armstrang', 'Kinmont Willie', 'The Ballad of Johnny Faa', and hundreds of others record the sometimes heroic, often cruel and dishonourable exploits and fates of real-life personages, in vivid, anonymous poetry.

Not content only to collect, however, Sir Walter Scott felt obliged to touch these traditional songs here and there with his own poetic gift, rectifying their orthography, and occasionally altering the meaning for a more genteel readership. To give but one example, in the ballad 'The Dowie Dens o' Yarrow', he changed Scots words such as 'gaed' and 'houms' to 'sped' and 'banks', and re-wrote the line, 'She drank the red bluid frae him ran' to the less immediate and less original, 'She kissed him, till her lips grew red'. He also interpolated a number of 'poetic' words, such as 'oft' and 'noble', to suit, so he wrote, 'the taste of "these more light and giddy-paced times"'.

The *Minstrelsy* was Scott's first book and the first step in the role he was to make his own, as publicist for Scotland. It is not just modern scholars who have objected to his 'editing'; Margaret Laidlaw, a ballad singer and the mother of James Hogg, issued an instant rebuke:

There was never ane o' ma sangs prentit till ye prentit them yoursel, and ye hae spoiled them althegither. They were made for singing and no for reading, but ye hae broken the charm now, and they'll never be sung mair. And the worst thing o' a'; they're neither right spell'd nor right setten down.

★ ★ ★

On the fifth morning of my stay, the landlord at Maxwellheugh came into my room without knocking before I had dressed and announced that they would be shifting me into a caravan immediately after breakfast, as the joiners were moving in.

I settled up and left.

I spent a boring night in Ettrickbridge, a small village beyond Selkirk. The most exciting moment of my stay was when a local man spilled a pint of beer over my knees.

Next morning I waited for a lift to take me back to Selkirk, where I could catch a bus going south towards Langholm. The landscape of the Ettrick Valley suited me, mostly green pastures and soft hills, arranged neatly, but without primness, everywhere refreshed by burns and rivers.

It rained sporadically but I tried not to allow that to affect my temper. 'In Scotland,' remarked the Californian wife of Robert Louis Stevenson, 'a fair day appears to mean fairly wet. "It is quite fair now," they will say, when you can hardly distinguish the houses across the street.'

On some roads there are few cars, and on this one I waited an hour. It was the last day of June, 'quite fair' and I was wet. During a dry patch, when the sun glowed above a silver-grey bank of cloud, a farmer stopped and picked me up, smiling out from under the brim of his floppy tweed hat.

'No such a bad day,' he said while I dripped dry.

After that, he broke the silence only once to point out the house where Mungo Park, the African explorer, was born, and told me to look out for the statute in Selkirk outside his father-in-law's grander house, which showed Mungo being fed by an African woman who found him destitute after he had escaped some kidnappers.

'The days'll be gettin' shorter now,' he concluded as we reached our destination.

Approaching the Market Place, dominated by the statue of Scott who spent thirty-three years here as sheriff, I heard more music – a lone piper was playing 'Scotland the Brave'. For a few moments I was host to the irrepressible romantic illusion, of the charm unbroken. After a few bars, the tune stumbled through a purgatory of discord and then emerged as 'Flower of Scotland', a recently publicised alternative national anthem for the 'new Scotland'.

Increasing my pace, I reached the top of the hill and came into the Place, face to face with a kilted piper marching on the spot. Behind him stood a white caravan bedecked with tartan bunting and posters of soldiers recommending a life in the army. The tune changed again, this time to 'Amazing Grace', to which a teenage girl beside me began singing along.

I accepted a leaflet from a uniformed officer in trousers, enjoining me to travel and defend my country.

2

Curst Conceit

In the morning a smirr of rain lasted until just after noon, when the clouds broke; they opened, shut, then opened again, in a pattern which continued for the rest of the day.

I stepped down from the bus opposite the new Post Office in Langholm, deep in Eskdale. It is a compact town, built on the banks of the River Esk, and situated six miles from the border at a point where the Esk, Ewes and Wauchope waters meet.

In the café next to the bus-stop, I ordered a cup of tea at the counter. Some schoolchildren and Langholm's single tramp were the only other customers. A juke box vied for attention with rattling video games. I drank the milky tea quickly and wondered if I should stop here or continue. I had chosen it for a brief stopover only because of its connection with the poet Hugh MacDiarmid, Scotland's sole undisputed twentieth-century literary genius, who was born here, but suddenly that did not seem a good enough reason.

The juke box was fed and began to belt out its inscrutable rhythms. Two schoolboys celebrated their electronic destructive powers. The tramp dozed off. I stood up and left, and outside pondered a purring bus with 'Carlisle' posted on the front.

But it rumbled away before I reached a decision, and so in the meantime I crossed the River Esk and hid my bag in the church, beneath a pew, then started walking in the direction of the Border.

★   ★   ★

These are called the 'Debateable Lands'. Before the stability which followed the Union of the Crowns in 1603, the shaky line separating

Scotland from England was frequently in question and in constant need of protection, if not reclamation. As well as being among Scotland's finest poetry, the ballads which emanate from this territory constitute a vivid record of how the area felt in the Middle Ages when the authority of Border chieftains rivalled, and even surpassed, that of the King.

One of the most famous ballads tells the story of Johnie Armstrang, a Robin Hood figure of both history and legend, in whom King James v saw a potential usurper. According to the ballad, Johnie was eventually summoned to the King's presence by a 'luving letter', which he treated as an honour, and arrived to keep his appointment dressed in finery, with a company of his best men. The King realised the success of his scheme, took them prisoner, and with his men Johnie was hanged at Carlinrig in or about 1530.

> John was murdered at Carlinrigg,
> And all his gallant cumpanie;
> But Scotland's heart was never sae wae
> To see sae mony brave men die.
>
> Because they saved their country deir
> Frae Englishmen; nane were sae bauld
> While Johnie lived on the Border syde,
> Nane of them durst come neir his hauld.

There is naturally much debate in the history books about whether the reivers really were friends to the poor, or merely self-aggrandising thieves, stealing from those who might have been counted among their own folk, as well as from their enemies. Official records give one side of the story – the King's – and the ballads, which could be called the record of popular feeling, give another. The Border ballads affirm the Scots' attachment to folk heroes, in particular those who strike a blow against their traditional English oppressors, and the 'Ballad of Johnie Armstrang' illustrates the willingness of the Scots to put their faith in popular leaders before noble ones, a notable aspect of Scottish democracy.

In the nineteenth-century Highlands, the supplanting of the traditional clan system by a group of wealthy landowners, some of whom had little or no Scottish connections (and those who had soon forsook them), aided the process of romanticisation of the Highlander and his native habitat. The Borders, on the other hand, perhaps because it has retained its population as the Highlands has not, has largely resisted the excesses of the 'publicists for Scotland'.

But not entirely.

Johnie Armstrang's tower at Gilnockie (also known as Hollows Tower) is still standing, one of many in the Borders, above a waterfall on the River Esk. It is in most respects like every other peel tower: a massive, turreted, monolithic matchbox, with a false suggestion that it once belonged to a more elaborate structure. The walls are six feet thick in places and there is a vaulted ceiling above the ground floor. The upper storeys are reached by a stone wheel-stair which was built with the rest of the tower in 1518. The whole is fashioned to withstand the warring approaches of enemies like Lord Dacres, Warden of the English Marches, who burned it in 1528. At the apex of the south gable is a beacon stand in which fires were lit to warn of the approach of hostile forces and rally the clan. The entrance to the vaulted chamber has an interesting door still bearing spiral and other markings. It is a burial stone of the Bronze Age, 3,000 years old. The first floor is the Great Hall and has a massive open fireplace. There are stone seats in the window openings. On the second floor is the 'Laird's Room' which has a garde-robe, or privy en suite.

I quote from a leaflet issued, and probably written, by the occupant. In one respect the tower of the legendary Border reiver who was deceived and hanged without ceremony from a tree at Carlinrig is different from every other one: it is restored and inhabited – and all done by a man called Armstrong.

As he let me down at the end of the long path leading to the tower, the bus driver pointed to a large 'For Sale' sign posted by the door.

'You'll be wantin' to buy it.'

I then noticed a smaller sign which said that visitors would be received by appointment only. I was in the middle of a country road, and, on checking, found no telephone at the cluster of houses half a mile further on. Anyway, I reasoned, the owner would be unlikely to invite me in at such short notice. The leaflet, which described the tower as equally a museum and a house, had said nothing about this.

The only thing to do was to knock on the door and see what happened.

My hand was raised when the low, wooden door opened inwards. Crouched in it was a thin-faced, aristocratic-looking man, who proved to be extremely tall when he stood up to his full height, with a watering can in his hand. The new Laird of Gilnockie looked surprised, and then displeased, to see me. Hastily, I improvised on the suggestion that I was considering writing something about the area.

'You are? Ah!. . . Do come in.'

He put the watering can at his feet and retreated into the dark interior, ducking as he passed from one room to another. I followed, to the room which serves as kitchen and living room. It was artificially lighted, since the small windows permit scarce natural light, with a massive barrel vault overhead. There was a damp smell from the stone walls reminiscent of ruined castles, but so faint in this instance that the Laird and his wife would have long ago ceased to notice it. He apologised for the mess, though only in the way that people do, since it was actually tidy, explaining that he had just returned from an expedition to the now uninhabited island of St Kilda, some hundred and ten miles off the north-west coast.

His restoration work was truly extraordinary: ceilings, floors, fireplaces, walls, on several storeys, all had to be expertly treated, before interior fitments could even be considered.

'Was it a ruin when you bought it?'

'You could see the sky above from this spot when I first came here. The fireplaces were still in place, but only as shells. The whole of this vault here had to be restored as well.'

'Was it expensive?'

'You can imagine – or rather, you can't! I wouldn't think the local builder in Langholm could have tackled this lot, would you?'

Why did he do it?

'It was fun.'

But not only for fun. Major S. Armstrong-Simpson, who was born across the border, believes he is a direct descendant of Johnie Armstrang. The Armstrong clan is a 'broken' one, that is a clan which has no chief; and so his decision to restore the home of one of its most famous sons to something resembling its original condition, was taken out of a sense of duty.

'I felt I had a responsibility to Johnie, and to the Armstrong clan. But I reached the final decision with my wife, because of the interest we both share in history and in old buildings.'

Some historians portray Johnie as an outlaw and thief, rather than the Robin Hood figure of legend; Scott, working from historical sources, wrote that he 'spread terror', and, referring to his 'evil genius', noted that he 'levied black-mail'; the Major's own publicity notes that the word entered the language through the reivers' success in extracting it from Borders landowners in return for 'protection'. There is even an expression, 'Elliots and Armstrongs ride thieves all'.

Major Armstrong-Simpson rejected this version.

'Johnie was a very . . . *gentle* man, a very trusting man. He was a kind-hearted person who robbed the rich only to give to the poor.'

'He appears to have been quite well off himself,' I said, surprised to hear myself discussing this shadowy personage in familiar terms.

'Yes, he had to keep up a certain style, as all leaders do, but there never was an element of self-aggrandisement about his accumulation of wealth and property. He was devoted to his people, as they were to him.'

I was about to ask if the rich of the day took it in such good part as, presumably, Major Armstrong-Simpson would have done, when he offered to show me the upper floors. On the second storey he led me to a small square window with a splendid new frame in place.

'This is where the ladies looked out and saw their men riding away to keep their fateful appointment with the King, whom they met in good faith, of course. They were dressed in all their finery and one of the women cried out' – he cupped his hands around his mouth – '"God bring our men back well again!" It was the last time they saw them alive.'

On the top floor, a small, low-ceilinged room had been converted into a showplace for prints of the tower in its prerestoration state, and various gimcrack souvenirs, such as car stickers with 'Glinockie Tower' written on them, badges, and little model aluminium Glinockie Towers, were for sale. Side by side with these were photo graphs and souvenirs of another of Major Armstrong-Simpson's heroes, the American astronaut and first man on the moon, Neil Armstrong, who visited Langholm in 1972. There were some badges for sale with spaceships on them.

Downstairs again, his wife joined us. With coffee and cigarette, she told me of their regret at having to sell the place. The expense of restoration, plus rates, had proved too much. As conversation started up between the two of them, I looked for an opening to excuse myself. Mention was made of a recent royal garden party on the lawn of Holyrood House, the Queen's residence in Edinburgh, which they had attended. Resentment of royalty among the Armstrongs, I joked, had not persisted to the present day, then?

I stood up and thanked the Major for having received me unannounced. A curious place, a curious life, to live among some relics and a legend. Only a strong sense of romance, he freely acknowledged, permitted him to believe that his line went right back to Johnie of the ballad.

'We have to rely a lot on guesswork, it has to be said. But research is continuing all the time into the Armstrong line. It's probable that a new chief will be appointed quite soon by the Lord Lyon in Edinburgh.'

'Will you be putting yourself forward?'

'Not likely! Haven't the time, what with this place to look after.'

He saw me to the door.

'The strange thing is,' I mumbled as I emerged from the artificially lighted tower, 'you're not even a Scot yourself.'

'Ah! You're not the first to say that. But I've always felt Scottish. My wife and I have always loved the Scottish countryside and long before we bought this place we had wanted to come here. And it's in my blood – it's as simple as that. I often wear the kilt and play the bagpipes. You saw the set of pipes upstairs? . . . '

He had pointed out the red velvet bag, obviously draped for effect across a chair of a different period from the other furniture, and told me that they used to belong to Queen Victoria and came from Balmoral, that the Queen's manservant, John Brown, would play a tune on them for her every day. I had asked him for a tune there and then, but he'd declined.

'But I do play them,' he said. 'I play them every day, almost. I love the skirl of the pipes on a misty morning better than I love any other sound in the whole, wide world. It reminds me that deep, deep down, I *am* Scottish.'

II

A stetson-hatted angler from Bradford rocketed me back to Langholm. From a nest of beer cans on the back seat, he handed one to me and unzipped another for himself. He first came here in 1965, he told me, almost colliding with a small bicyclist, and had been coming back every year since. The fishing was great, but the people were 'loco'.

From its place beneath the pew, I retrieved my bag and booked into the Buck Hotel for a night. Its stained dark wood panelling and brass fittings were as they had been at the beginning of the century. It was not the only hotel on Langholm's banana-shaped main street, but it looked the most inviting and a small square of paper pinned to the door-jamb spared me the potential embarrassment of being put off by the price: 'Bed & Breakfast £7.50'.

As the only guest that night I was given a spacious double room with a large brass bed and a handsome suite of stripped pine. When the wind started up, it howled in the chimney. After settling in, I sat on the bed to read a book.

The solitary traveller anticipates long wastes of time which he can bridge with books, but I found it difficult to tackle any serious reading, with so many distractions in the strange world outside. So far, I had flicked through Tomson's *Border Ballads*, but had looked at nothing else.

What books to take on a journey? With the best of intentions, I had brought a copy of *The Heart of Midlothian*, but knew already that I would not be picking it up again. I had packed some non-fiction too: a book about horse racing published in America, and Graham Greene's *The Lawless Roads*, an account of his journey into Mexico in the 1930s during the country's brutal religious purges. The title derives from a poem by Edwin Muir: 'without fear the lawless roads/Ran wrong all through the land.' With the author's other

books in the same genre, it has become a classic of modern travel
writing. I opened it and read some, but after ten minutes put it away.
It was too good. Greene's drama of human endeavour in a theatre of
futility found me willing as ever. But I found his tone, of one talking
to his best friend, too intimate, and fatally imitable.

Also weighing me down was one basic guide book – Muirhead's
of 1927, updated by John Tomes – a variety of periodicals, and one or
two other books, including a library copy of Hugh MacDiarmid's
Penny Wheep (1926) which was fast accumulating fines. Finally, I
settled for that.

> I met ayont the cairney
> A lass wi' tousie hair
> Singin' till a bairnie
> That was nae langer there.
>
> Wunds wi' warlds to swing
> Dinna sing sae sweet,
> The licht that bends owre a'thing
> Is less ta'en up wi't.

The main impetus behind this poetry is the most coherent Scottish
literary tradition – the Ballads. By reviving it, MacDiarmid was not
only borrowing tried and tested modes, he was attempting to draw
some of its coherence into his own world. The dialect in these poems
is not 'pure', does not originate from a single, limited geographical
area, but was created by MacDiarmid by the unusual method of
plundering old Scots dictionaries in search of words which would
suit his purpose, taken from different dialects, resulting in what is
called 'synthetic Scots'. His writing was only the most durable
aspect of a gigantic effort to reunite a nation and a culture which had
gone adrift, to repair a charm which had been broken.

He was born the son of a postman in 1892, in a house below the
library left to the town by Thomas Telford, the engineer, the earlier
famous son. In a typical piece of exaggeration, MacDiarmid claimed
to have read every one of its twelve thousand books by the age of
fourteen: a feat which would have involved reading about twenty a
week, starting at the age of four. Nevertheless, he was a man of
prodigious energy: besides his literary activities, which were

multifarious and resulted in some eighty books, he worked with the Independent Labour Party and the Fabian Research Department at the same time as studying to be a teacher; then, in Montrose, where he later lived, he was a journalist, Labour Councillor and Justice of the Peace; he was a crofter in Shetland, and afterwards a fitter on the Clyde; and he lent his name to many political causes (some of which had no wish of him) including Communism and Scottish Nationalism.

MacDiarmid's personality is so demanding, that I must have been expecting it to leap out and meet me the moment I stepped down in Langholm. Instead, all I recognised was the monotonous peacefulness common to all Scottish small towns, which in the evening turns to eerie silence, punctuated by the sounds of children and drunks.

★   ★   ★

I went into a public bar and ordered a pint of beer. The barman nodded a grim welcome but ignored my request until he finished pouring a pint of Guinness. He walked slowly up to the far end of the bar to deliver it, proudly inspecting it and setting it down as if it were a piece of sculpture. Then he returned to attend to me. I gave him the opportunity to create another one.

'Am I right in thinking this is where Hugh MacDiarmid came from?' I asked tentatively.

'Aye . . . ' He nodded again, without raising his eyes from the latest work of art which was just coming to fruition under his fingers. 'That's right, isn't it, Archie? Archie there'll tell you. Hugh MacDiarmid – the poet?'

Archie was a very small man with a large cap and was holding a whippet on a length of string. He let his eyes close as he nodded authoritatively.

The barman skimmed the creamy top with a flat bone and set the pint on the bar before me.

'They're puttin' up a monument to him, I heard,' he said, throwing a crust to the dog.

'What sort of monument?'

'I dinna ken, son. Ask Archie.'

Archie deliberated for a moment, trying to decide if he should pretend to know more than he did. Finally, he came down on the side of candour.

'Ask in the Tourist Office,' he said. 'The fella in there'll tell you.' 'I heard he had an uneasy relationship with the place. Is that right?' 'He said he wouldna take the freedom of the town,' Archie said. 'And that was afore they offered it to him.'

'And he wrote in one o' his books that attendance at Langholm Academy was a dubious privilege,' the barman chimed in. 'Well, any man that says that aboot his own school canna expect to be honoured by the toon.'

'Have you seen his grave yet?' asked Archie, and then he surprised us all by quoting its inscription in full voice:

> 'I'll ha'e nae hauf-way hoose, but aye be whaur
> Extremes meet – it's the only way I ken
> To dodge the curst conceit o' bein' richt
> That damns the vast majority o' men.'

There was a moment's silence, followed by a few drops of applause.

'You should hear Archie on Burns Night.'

'I read somewhere,' I said, 'that MacDiarmid asked for his inscription to be "A disgrace to the community".'

'Aye, so it should've been.' The barman threw another crust to the dog which responded eagerly.

* * *

In the morning, before the chambermaid-cum-manageress showed me into the large, empty dining room for breakfast, I slipped out to buy the *Scotsman*. The street had a fresh, welcoming, early-morning feel to it, shopkeepers were washing their steps, the occasional motor car chugged along the main street, and people I passed greeted me as if they had been used to doing so every morning of their lives.

After breakfast, I set off to hitch-hike west, there being no buses. I crossed the Esk and walked to the boundary, past a sheepskin factory with a devilish stink. The first car to come along looked full, but I stuck out a thumb and it stopped. Two girls, a mother and a grandmother who was driving, reshuffled themselves and suddenly there was a space for me.

They were on their way to harvest a gooseberry patch some miles outside the town. Casually, I asked for their opinion of Langholm's latest famous son, half-expecting a blank response. Instead, howls of disapproval filled the overloaded car.

'We're no fans!' bawled the elder girl.

'Why not?'

'He was always against Burns.'

'He was a communist,' said the grandmother from the wheel; she repeated this charge at every available interval.

'Was that the only reason?'

'He was always sayin' things to put Burns down,' said the girl again. It transpired that she had certificates for recitation of Burns's poetry, and was a keen collector of his work. They talked enthusiastically of certain poems, quoting liberally; the grandmother said she knew a very old man who owned a first Kilmarnock edition of Burns's *Poems Chiefly in the Scottish Dialect*. 'I don't think he'll last much longer,' she said. 'I'm hopin' he'll leave it to me.' Then she said again: 'MacDiarmid was a communist.'

'But surely it's possible to like MacDiarmid *and* Burns?'

'We canny understand his poetry,' said the old woman, reminding me of MacDiarmid's self-contradictory boast that he wrote in a 'linguistic medium unintelligible to "the mob"'.

'I heard they're putting up a monument to him.'

'We'll tear it down!'

Soon afterwards, they reached their destination, a point without landmarks along a narrow road with uncultivated fields on both sides, which only the familiar eye could have recognised. We all spilled out and they climbed through the wire fence, baskets in hand, and waded through the barley towards the gooseberries. The mother remained behind and, without consulting me, flagged down another car and more or less ordered its owner to drive me to the next town. With a reluctance she made no attempt to hide, the new driver agreed, leaving me embarrassed but helpless to resist.

'I don't normally stop for people,' she charged me as we set off, ignoring my incoherent, half-sincere apology about the total absence of public transport, and that the request for her to stop was not mine. 'Since you're only going a mile or two . . . '

She was a horsy woman who had married into money in Langholm. I asked what she thought of Hugh MacDiarmid. She had never heard of him.

'He was a poet,' I said. 'And he was a communist. And also a Scottish Nationalist.'

'Oh.'

'He's the only person ever to have been expelled from the Communist Party for being a Scottish Nationalist, and from the Scottish National Party for being a communist.'

'I think I *have* heard of him, now that you mention it,' she said, but I did not believe her.

3
The Big Idea

I spent over an hour looking for a place to stay in Dundee. After one night in Dumfries, a series of buses ferried me northwards, through Edinburgh. Every bus station where I had to change had a feeling of lethargic despair about it; families who had intended to make their holiday voyages by train had had to change plans suddenly, because of the continuing rail strike, and long queues coiled round the insides of booking offices and poked their tails outside.

In Edinburgh I had asked about the express bus to Dundee. The booking clerk regarded me with impatient scorn.

'Listen, you've got more chance of a job *driving* the thing than you have of getting a seat now. So what else can I do for you?'

It meant taking a local bus to Dunfermline, then another to Perth, and yet another to Dundee; four hours to cover some sixty miles.

The traveller who enters Dundee by rail from south of the River Tay would have a spectacular view from the train as it crosses the railway bridge, which curves like an ice-hockey stick, before running along the bank to the station. Set on a crop of volcanic rock, the heights of Dundee offer a bold prospect.

When I arrived it was raining heavily. Most of the cheap bed and breakfast places I tried were full, or else would not accept a single boarder, as the Queen Mother was in town for a graduation ceremony at Dundee University next day. Eventually, I found one. It had a piece of card tied to the railing outside, with 'Acomodation £4, 50' heavily pencilled on it.

'On your way to Aberdeen?' the landlady asked, without a trace of irony or bruised pride. I said yes, I would be going that way later on.

My reason, though, was clearly different from the one she had in mind; she was talking about oil and money. It is a poignant comment on the relationship between the two cities nowadays that many Dundonians should think of theirs only as the temporary stopping-place for fortune-hunters.

I climbed the stairs behind the landlady, to go through the ceremony of viewing the room – somewhat unnecessarily, since I would be bound to take it unless it resembled a pigsty.

Unfortunately, it did.

The door swung wide to reveal the most miserable place I had ever seen. The wallpaper was brown and peeling, the ceiling was cracked in the corners, the carpet was long unswept; a pathetic attempt had been made to decorate the walls with cheap prints of coloured humming birds; in the middle of the floor sat a swivel chair whose seat was detached from its base. For light, there was only a small skylight window without an inner frame, and there were shelves tightly packed with spare blankets and two or three rolled-up gaberdine raincoats.

She held the door open while I peered through the gloom and tried to arrange my reactions of resignation and disgust. The thought of setting out again, in this weather, with a bag which put on several pounds each time I picked it up, made me even weaker than I really was. The house was silent. In my despair I suspected her of having a vacant, immaculate room somewhere deep inside this large house, and that she was trading off these filthy places one by one, until her ideal customer came along.

'Is this all right for you?'

'You haven't got another chair, by any chance?'

'Why, do you want to sit down?'

I could have used the bed (it sagged murderously and that night I slept on the floor) but she called to a young man who arrived from downstairs and then, on her instructions, went into the room next to mine and returned with a hard dining-room chair. Then they left, insisting that if I needed anything I should not hesitate to sing out for it. I assured her I would. Hearing the kitchen door close behind them, I sneaked downstairs and emerged into the damp, grey streets with a truant's guilty relief.

The young man – he was not her son – was one of a type quite common in guest houses run by mature landladies. They change the sheets and sweep the carpets in exchange for board. This one cooked my breakfast next morning, and informed me at length, while the bacon burned to a crisp, that it was better than working.

*　　*　　*

Dundee was not working. Industrial cities like it have suffered most from an industrial recession which is universal. The effects of such withdrawal are particularly cruel when a town's indigenous manufactures are at stake. Dundee's industries – 'jute, jam and journalism' is the convenient formula – were its *raison d'être*; in effect, they bore the city as it stands today and without them the community, and the culture which stems from it, stand in disarray. Moreover, the industries of 'the future' were in trouble already. While I was staying in Dundee, what proved to be a protracted battle between management and unions at a large electronics works was just beginning. Jobs for 2,200 workers were dissolving from an enterprise which had been one of the brightest hopes for the future, which had promised to help build a new Dundee. Now newspapers were calling it 'Crisis City', and an instant curse was issued by the city fathers upon the head of every journalist who said as much. In defiant letters to the press, they espoused their good intentions, plans and designs, while the battle for the 2,200 jobs took place above their heads. The enemy was being commanded from a long way off.

I took a walk round the Dundee of the past.

There are still a number of jute mills in Dundee; almost all are derelict. The largest is Baxter's Mills in Princes Street, a factory spread over an area of nine acres – the size of a small village. Built in the nineteenth century as the linen industry approached its peak, its design reflects a grand purpose and an unassailable faith in 'progress'. The façade contains features borrowed from Italian Renaissance palaces, and from the central pediment a statue of James Watt, who patented his steam engine in 1769, once presided over the workers arriving at the factory in the morning. Baxter Brothers' trade mark was HMS *Victory*, Nelson's ship at Trafalgar, for which the firm produced the canvas. Its independent existence came to an end in

1924, when it was taken over by the firm of Law and Bonar, and although the linen industry enjoyed a revival in this century because of the effects of war, its high point had been reached by the end of the last. The ruined mills of the Dens Works in Princes Street are a monument to the city's former importance in the Empire, and are now a popular tourist attraction.

I walked round the outside of the mills. Old signs still in place added a simple, personal touch: 'Staff Only'; 'All Visitors Must Report To – '; 'Canteen First Floor' . . .

Finding a side-door open, I looked over my shoulder in case anyone was watching, and then slipped inside. It was just a large office overlooking the factory floor, where machine fitments sprouted from the walls. I was hoping for the poetic detail which would illuminate the experience of inspecting this museum but came away disappointed. It was a prosaic dereliction.

*　*　*

Mrs Gibbs dragged at a Capstan Full Strength and with the other hand speared a rasher of bacon. She had strong views on most things, and insisted on detaining me with some of them while I attempted to pay for my night's stay.

'Education's a great thing, you know.'

'Yes, I agree.'

'A command of the English language – that's what I would wish for if I had a wish. The gift of words. It's a great thing.'

I held out the five pound note but she ignored it.

'See with words, you can do anything. When I was in Africa, see the notes I took – if I had an education, a command of the English language, I could have wrote a great book.'

I kept my eyes on the clock behind her head. She had lived in Rhodesia before it became Zimbabwe and strongly favoured the black government there.

'That's what we need in this country, some forward-looking men. Are you with me?'

'Yes.' I put the money on the table and explained that I had to hurry, I had an interview with the Chairman of the Scottish National Party, Gordon Wilson, and already it was close to the appointed time.

'Oh, Wilson, he's a decent man. Not a leader but a good man. I like him. I don't support the SNP, you understand, but I think Wilson's a good constituency MP. What are you going to ask him?'

'Just general things.'

'See if I gave you my notes, you could write a best-seller.'

From the corner of my eye I could see the energetic young permanent resident changing sheets and pillow cases in the downstairs bedroom which I surmised they shared. She stubbed out the cigarette, lit another, and sat back in her chair again, eager to tell me more.

II

'We need self-government because we *are* a nation, that's why.'

Gordon Wilson's answer to my first question – what would you tell a man from Africa who asked why Scotland should have independence? – was totally convinced.

'You can tell me that Scotland is a part of the United Kingdom, and I will tell you that that is the truth but not the whole truth.' He paused and smiled, confident in his own living room which faced the small and tidy front garden, and with an answer and question which had both been spoken many times before.

'You see, national boundaries are not simply a matter of geographical frontiers. It's culture we're talking about, a set of national characteristics. These Scotland has retained, but she has not had the chance to develop them as she deserves.'

He is a slight, bright-eyed man, with sloping shoulders, a haircut of military severity, boyish features and a cheerful manner. Under his leadership, since 1979 (the year of the disastrous referendum on the establishing of a Scottish Assembly), the SNP had come out in favour of total independence. It would be prepared to share certain services, such as the armed forces, with Westminster, but would prefer to bargain for these concessions from a position of what Mr Wilson called 'one hundred per cent'.

The party was going through a period of rough weather when we met, from which the Chairman was striving to save it. Some infighting between a breakaway left-wing group and the party at large had almost ruined the SNP, but now, thanks to Wilson's action, was on the point of being resolved. The problem of declining public support was not, however. Until the failure of the referendum, the SNP had thrived in the nationalist atmosphere which intensified during the seventies, and as it grew in strength by the season there seemed a real chance that it would one day achieve a majority in the Westminster parliament within Scotland. However, at the general election which followed the referendum, nine nationalist MPs lost their seats, leaving only two – Gordon Wilson and one other. (A position which remained the same after the election of June 1983.) The prime of SNP life looked as if it might be over.

'Not at all. As I said, Scotland has not had the chance to develop her national characteristics in the past, and now she deserves the chance to do so. This, we believe, can only be done through self-government, and self-government can only be achieved by putting pressure on the present administration and persuading them that the Scottish people want it. Which party is in a position to do this? The SNP.'

'But you only have two MPs.'

Mr Wilson was prepared and did not flinch.

'In 1979 we were reduced from eleven members to two, it is true. But politics goes in dips, which is what you must try to understand. That is what lost us the referendum. 1977–8 was our best period, in terms of public support, not the following year, when the referendum was held. Had we had the referendum the year before, we believe we would have gained a large enough majority, with votes enough to spare. Anyway, you mustn't forget that the SNP was not wholly in favour of the terms of the Scottish Assembly, as set out in the government's White Paper. I myself was tempted not to vote for it because it didn't go far enough.'

'Is your party heading for a revival?'

'It would be a poor leader who answered no to that one, wouldn't it?' He smiled. 'But yes – definitely. I would estimate that if there were an election tomorrow we could gain between three and five MPs – that's *gain*. No more than that. But in twelve to eighteen months, who knows? Eighteen months is a long time in politics. We **are** optimistic, and we hold to our belief that eventually the Scottish people will vote for us to show that they want control of their own affairs.'

'Has Scotland benefited in any way from the oil discovered off its shores?'

'Not at all. There has been some improvement in local prosperity – that's all.'

'Is oil necessary to the success of an independent Scotland?'

'No. And this is important. Even without oil, the Scottish economy could manage itself better than it is presently managed from down south. What you must understand is that economic centralisation causes distortions in the economy of *this* country. It is at the root of our severe unemployment. In an independent Scotland, high unemployment would not be the inevitability it has become under Westminster. Read our policy document on "Manpower and Industrial Relations". If you make the comparison with Norway which has a population similar to ours, you'll see what we could achieve here. Norway has three per cent unemployment; ours is four times that much.'

'Can the SNP promise that kind of improvement?'

'Read our policy document on "Post-Independence Economic Strategy."'

Later on, I read the policy documents, small booklets comprising a few sheets stapled together, frequently stumbling over phrases such as 'In an independent Scotland . . . ', 'Under independence . . . ', followed by a combination of familiar political rhetoric and cheerful optimism of a kind available only to politicians who depend on never attaining power. Indeed, the rhetoric is only made to appear more absurd by being uttered from a state of impotence. The SNP and their supporters claim that the party exists to cure that impotence, but it is more likely that it has been disabled by it. The policy documents which I read – the most up-to-date statements of the aims of the SNP available – were written on average six years earlier.

On the achievement of independence, measures will be adopted which will become immediately effective in attaining the following objectives:

(i) A dramatic reduction in our appalling and intolerable level of unemployment

(ii) An attack on inflation to stabilise prices with the help of a strong Scottish pound

(iii) Aid and encouragement to native enterprise in both manufacturing and resource development, particularly in sectors of replaceable imports, with the help of decentralised development offices . . .

On the achievement of independence measures will be immediately adopted which will have an increasing effect in the longer term in attaining the following objectives:

(i) The radical restructuring and upgrading of Scottish industry in the light of world market conditions and prospects

(ii) In order to obtain the objectives of full employment, job satisfaction, rising living standards and shorter working hours, it will be essential for the Scottish Government to promote improved productivity in the economy as a whole . . .

And so on: 'modernisation of the economic infrastructure', 'more flexibility between public and private enterprise, a better balance between international and indigenous companies', 'encouragement of good industrial relations', 'increased employee participation in enterprise policy-making', 'a programme of food and energy production and utilisation coupled with conservation and recycling where appropriate', 'the expansion of rural communities' – the policy documents, years out of date, promised the best of all possible worlds, in unpunctuated rhetoric which even the Chairman made little effort to defend.

'Is the SNP running out of ideas?'

'Certainly not. There may be a bit of post–79 depression floating about, but you'll never take the big idea away from us. The big idea is still there.'

III

The sign on the front of the bus read 'Blairgowrie', which had a pleasing Highland ring to it, although I was travelling with the bus less than fifteen miles furth of Dundee.

The majority of my fellow passengers were elderly. Outside

Dundee, a family piled on – mother and father, children, grand-parents, the dog, and some odd bits and pieces which could have been in-laws or cousins. The driver of the bus grew impatient with the father's attempts to squeeze all their suitcases and plastic bags and a collapsible pram into the small interior luggage compart-ment, but made no move to help, only hampering the man further by jolting the bus into motion before his belongings were stowed away. They stood in a line along the corridor and one of the unnameable lit a cigarette in the 'No Smoking' section, which brought glances, but no words, from the two seriously hatted ladies in front of me.

Only a few miles on, they got off, ejecting themselves with a similar delay, and set everyone in the bus talking.

The sky was blue and brilliant at last, though I noticed when I stepped down from the bus at the Kinloch Arms in Meigle that the grass betrayed rain from the night before. Now, however, there was not a hint of breeze to worry the barley. It was growing hot, and the July heat would last all the way up the east coast to the height of Scotland.

I was on Balhary Estate. I walked about a mile from the bus-stop to the lodge, past the house itself, where Gerry Mangan met me at the door. All week he worked at his painting and writing, and this was the one day when he performed some odd jobs for the owners of the estate, the Misses Kinloch-Smyth, in lieu of rent for the lodge.

Before he started, we sat on the Victorian park bench which somehow had found its way on to the small, square, sloping lawn adjacent to the lodge house. There was no one in sight. The lodge house is posted on the old road, almost unused now and well behind the main road between Dundee and Blairgowrie.

All of the land in our view would at one time have been owned by either of two families of local importance, the Kinlochs and the Smyths, whose connections by blood were well established before the marriage of Helen Smyth of Balhary to George Kinloch in 1796. The residence of Gerry's elderly employers, the present family seat, was built twenty-one years later while George Kinloch was headed for serious trouble with the law, but he and his wife never occupied never occupied it: through the strath, across the River Isla, scarcely visible, was Kinloch House, seat of one of nineteenth-century Dundee's most important men, now a hotel.

I went with Gerry as he walked to work at Balhary. The house itself is Georgian, in red sandstone, with some windows bricked up to evade Pitt's window tax, still in force at the time it was built. Raised on a slight artificial mound, the façade is pleasant but unremarkable. In the grounds immediately to the east of the house, however, there is something unusual – a prisoner-of-war camp.

It was built during World War II to house first German and then Italian prisoners who were brought to Scotland, and has simply never been demolished. Indeed, it stands remarkably intact, willing its own transformation into a symbol.

There are approximately fifty buildings, each one electrically wired and fitted with serviceable plumbing. In some places, nettles and weeds had grown higher than the windows, some rooms had been used to store bales of hay and bundles of old newspapers, and fungus had clogged the gutters and drains.

The entire complex was damp and smelly. Here and there, however, a human presence haunted it – for example, in the murals painted on each side of one of the doors, in a naive Renaissance style. One was of a Roman temple set among a thick bed of spruce trees, and the other was a mosque with a minaret in the foreground, suggesting that G. Felli – the artist who had left behind his signature – may have served in North Africa, before being brought to Balhary to live with the Misses Kinloch-Smyth, who got on very well with their charges. The local people, on the other hand, resented their doing work which they felt was by rights their own.

An earlier Kinloch, John (d. 1770), made his fortune in Jamaica, where he owned a sugar plantation. He built up a force of over 170 slaves, and in time added three of his own – two mulattos and one quadroon – who went into the field to work for their father.

This estate eventually passed to George Kinloch of Kinloch, the Radical Laird, whose statue stands in Dundee's Albert Square, wedged between Robert Burns and Queen Victoria, at the northern end of Reform Street, named after the cause for which he sacrificed his freedom.

The inscription on the statue reads:

George Kinloch
of Kinloch
outlawed for
the advocacy of popular rights
22 December 1819
Proclaimed member for Dundee
in the first reformed parliament
22 December 1832
Born Dundee 1775
Died London 1833
Erected by public subscription
to commemorate a signal triumph
of political justice
3 February 1872

Finding the ownership of slaves repugnant, George Kinloch sold the estate with its human assets, forecasting the end of the slave trade – a gesture characteristic of a man about to embark on a lifelong struggle on behalf of 'popular rights', in particular those of his beloved Dundonians, and the people's right to a representation in parliament.

At various times a Justice of the Peace, a Harbour Commissioner, landowner, reformer, instigator of the first passenger railway in Scotland, outlaw, and, finally, Member of Parliament for Dundee, George Kinloch enjoyed celebration and endured notoriety in his lifetime, but is almost forgotten today by the city and the nation for which he risked everything, and to whose development he contributed so much, in spite of the statue and a biography which allows the Radical Laird to speak for himself through his vigorous letters.

The earlier Kinlochs were not only slave traders. George's great-grandfather was imprisoned and sentenced to death (though later reprieved) for taking the Jacobite side in the Fifteen Rebellion and another Kinloch followed Prince Charles Edward Stuart and fought at Falkirk in 1746 (while an unwitting Duke of Cumberland stayed for a night at his house). Dr David Kinloch was granted part of the present estate in 1616 by King James VI and I, for having administered successful medical treatment. A branch of the family which moved to Somerset under the same monarch's reign produced A. W. Kinglake, the author of *Eothen* and *Invasion of the Crimea*. A later member of the family was a pre-Raphælite painter who lived in the Ardennes, where he shot the last wolf and became a local hero.

George Kinloch was orphaned in 1782, at the age of seven. He took to adventure early in life, crossing the Alps by mule before he was fifteen, and was in Dijon when the Bastille was stormed in 1789, which aroused his interest in contemporary France and its politics. Before settling down to the life of a country gentleman with Helen Smyth of Balhary, he attended university in Edinburgh, where he .dabbled (without graduating) in logic, maths, ethics and law. He was also a keen fiddle player. By all accounts, he was an honest employer, a good sportsman and a loyal and loving husband and father. Equally, he was conscious of his responsibilities as a landowner and one of the region's more privileged citizens, and it was in the course of discharging these duties that he made himself the enemy of Scotland's most powerful political men.

In 1814, Kinloch was promoting the idea of a new Harbour Board in Dundee. At the time, the harbour consisted of a small tidal basin, a breakwater of rubble and a wharf where both passengers and merchandise were brought ashore. The new, autonomous Harbour Commission – an autonomy much resented by the self-perpetuating Town Council, within which members elected themselves – was empowered to take control of Harbour Dues (which had been squandered by the Council) and to commission a design for a new harbour from Thomas Telford, without which the city could not have developed into a busy and important trading port.

Through this involvement, George Kinloch's political sympathies, practically dormant until then, came to life, and he became directly involved in the cause of the Rights of Man, particularly in the reform of the franchise. Such action by a landowner was not popular, either with Westminster, which kept a fearful eye on events across the Channel, or with Dundee's Town Council.

The passing of the Harbour Bill, divesting the Council of responsibility, was largely Kinloch's success, and was also the occasion for his adoption by the Guildry of Dundee as their champion. A report in the *Dundee Advertiser* on the celebrations for the success of the Harbour Bill made his commitment public:

> Mr Kinloch gave the toast of 'The Liberty and Independence of the Press, to which the inhabitants of this town have owed so much during the late discussions and may the Light which has burst upon us continue to expand until Corruption shall not have a hole wherein to hide its head.'
>
> He said, 'You have all, of late, had an arduous struggle which is not yet over but in which, if you continue firm and united . . . there can be no doubt of your ultimate success. There is another Corporation, of which we are all members and on all rights of which sad encroachments have been made . . . I mean the "Sovereign Rights of the People", and which I beg leave to propose a toast.'

This public display of his colours was eventually to cost him a great deal. Well within living memory Thomas Muir had been sentenced to fourteen years' transportation for sedition; at the same time several Dundonians were convicted on similar charges. Thomas Palmer received the same sentence as Muir for printing the text of an address on the subject of reform given by a methodist minister.

George Kinloch knew the risks he was running when he agreed to deliver a speech on the subject on Dundee's Magdalene Yard Green late in 1819. At first he hesitated over accepting the invitation, but the event which made up his mind was the Peterloo Massacre which took place in August of that year, when the Manchester Yeomanry charged a crowd of working people with bayonets, resulting in eleven deaths and countless injuries.

Ten thousand people assembled on the Green on 10 November to hear George Kinloch address them on 'the present STATE of the COUNTRY, with a view to suggest the means most likely to lead to a REFORM of ABUSES and an alleviation of the distress with which the working classes in particular are at present nearly overwhelmed'.

The speech itself was to the point:

> As to Universal Suffrage, seeing that all men are equal in the sight of their Creator, I cannot understand why one man should have a vote and another should not have one. Is not the life, the family, the property of the poor man as dear to him as the life, the property of the rich man is to him? . . .

The crowd responded with enthusiasm and dispersed peacefully.

With devious logic, however, the Lord Advocate in Edinburgh found proof of the Reformers' evil intentions in the good behaviour of the crowd. Addressing the House of Lords on the subject, he made the cute observation:

> Contrary to the nature of Scotsmen, 40,000 individuals will stand quietly for hours to hear the speeches of itinerant orators employed to corrupt them, and then disperse in the greatest order. This appears to me to denote some secret purpose on the part of the people.

In view of France, the country was nervous. Kinloch was charged with sedition and the combined talents of a trio of Edinburgh's best advocates – Jeffrey, Cranstoun and Cockburn – could not succeed in having the charge dropped. They felt as sure about the conviction as they did about the sentence – transportation – and the journey to Botany Bay was one which few made in reverse.

'Do you remember Kinloch of Kinloch who married a daughter of the very respectable Smyth of Balhary?' Sir Walter Scott wrote to a nephew on 9 December 1819. 'He is under indictment to stand trial in a few days for his conduct at a meeting of Radicals in Dundee, when he used the most inflammatory language which it seems he copied out in his own hand as well as the resolutions which were copied out in consequence. For much less matter was Muir in 1794 "doomed the long isles of Sydney Cove to see". The event of this trial will be very important.'

Scott, of course, was smacking his lips in anticipation of a conviction. His information was correct (allowing for the hyperbolic 'inflammatory language') except in one particular: George Kinloch would not be standing trial after all, for at three thirty on the very same morning that Scott had written to his nephew, he had boarded the Aberdeen Mail Coach for Edinburgh – the first step of a journey which led to more than three years' exile in Paris.

On the morning of 22 December – the date on his indictment to appear before the Criminal Court in Edinburgh – he stepped ashore in Calais. At the Mercat Cross in the High Street five hundred miles away, a Messenger at Arms blew three notes on a horn and denounced George Kinloch of Kinloch as an outlaw and a fugitive.

At first he enjoyed life in Paris, and his new status gave it added flavour.

> I have taken my abode here for the present. It is in Le Passage des Petits Pères behind the north east corner of the Palais Royal, in the most centrical part of Paris and my windows command a view of three streets . . . I have a parlour respectable enough for an *outlaw*, and a bed closet within it, and a place for my firewood. The dinner consists of soup, bouillé, a hash of some kind, fish, a roast, vegetables, apples and chestnuts . . . The company is all French except myself, an Englishman and a neat little English woman. I have the use of the salon all day and I make them light my fire about nine at night that I may retire to write or read.

He amused himself with a new clarinet, by giving lessons in French to the Englishwoman, and with long walks. Soon, however, this life became tiresome. His wife, Helen, and some of the children visited him with a view to staying, but there were health difficulties and they had to return. Then one of his daughters died before he had a chance to see her again.

In 1822, by which time the political climate had cooled, there was the hint of a pardon, and early in the following year the matter was settled. It was acknowledged that the action against him had been unnecessarily harsh and he was allowed to resume life in Strathmore, where he immediately took up his public duties again. He was instrumental in establishing the Dundee-Newtyle railway, a horse drawn service which was the first passenger line in the country, and which also made it easier to transport produce from the inland straths to Dundee for export.

Although his political activity was subdued, the cause of reform drew increased support over the next few years, culminating in the first Reform Bill of March 1831. In the elections which followed, George Kinloch's career achieved a just perfection: he was elected Member for Dundee in the first Reformed Parliament of 1832. His election had a pleasing neatness to it, which he did not fail to remark upon in the course of a speech at a celebration dinner organised in his honour by the electors of Dundee. On 22 December 1819, he had been proclaimed an outlaw at the Cross in Edinburgh as a result of the zeal of Sheriff L'Amy, who was 'hoping to make my shoulders a stepping stone to a certain bench, to which we know he would have added considerable weight'; now, on the same day thirteen years later, he was, by the same Sheriff L'Amy, being proclaimed the chosen representative in parliament of the people of Dundee.

Five months on, in a draughty room above a gunsmith's shop at 55 Parliament Street, London, George Kinloch of Kinloch died, having risen too soon from a fever in order to present some business in the House pertaining to Dundee – 'this great and flourishing community'.

* * *

He was not the only Scottish radical to suffer at that time, but in some ways he was the most remarkable and he does not deserve to have been obliterated by a history he helped to shape.

I asked everyone I met in Dundee if they had heard of him but no one had. Once, before I had located his statue, I asked someone about it. My acquaintance shook his head and thought for a few minutes before admitting that he could not help.

'You've heard about the statue they're putting up to McGonagall?'

I had not and did not find the news particularly cheering.

Sir William Topaz McGonagall, Poet and Tragedian, Knight of the White Elephant, Burmah – to use his full title – was a product of the machine age. He adopted the profession of letters late in life, and would not have done so at all had not the handloom weaving trade of which he was part been made redundant by the introduction of power mills to the city. He has become the Scottish stage poet, undoubtedly the most famous Scottish writer after Burns and Scott, the Caledonian equivalent of an Irish joke. His 'Poetic Gems' are masterpieces of talentlessness: no one could be so bad, marvels the reader, and still mean it. But McGonagall had complete faith in himself and never doubted for a moment his right to a place in the pantheon beside his two beloved masters, Burns and Shakespeare.

> The reason the Lords won't pass the Franchise Bill
> They fear it will do themselves some ill;
> That is the reason they wish to throw it out,
> Yes, believe me, fellow citizens, that's the cause without a doubt.

These are among the very few lines he ever wrote which would have evoked the sympathy of the Radical Laird. On the whole, he was a rigid conservative and monarchist. Usually he tackled big subjects – battles, great disasters, hymns in praise of public figures.

Oh! God, I thank thee for restoring King Edward the Seventh's health again,
And let all his subjects throughout the Empire say Amen;
May God guard him by night and by day,
At home and abroad, when he's far away.

Although now one of its most famous sons, McGonagall was treated badly by Dundee during his lifetime, and eventually was forced to leave the city as he had been prohibited from performing the dramatic renderings of his own verse from which he made a living. The reason given was that the spectacle caused over-excitement among the hooligan element in the audience which came to see him. This was hardly McGonagall's fault, but anyway the ban was made to stick, and the wretched poet was forced to move south, where the income from his readings, augmented by the benevolence of some kindly men, sustained him until his death in 1901.

As a young man the *Evening Times* journalist William Power witnessed a performance which McGonagall gave in the Albion Halls in Glasgow. He described a stooping man with long hair, which together with his athletic figure made him look younger than he really was. He entered the stage unshaven and dressed in a short kilt.

After reciting some of his own poems to an accompaniment of whistles and cat-calls, the Bard armed himself with a most dangerous-looking broadsword and strode up and down the platform declaiming 'Clarence's dream' and 'Give me another horse! – Bind up my wounds!' His voice rose to a howl. He thrust and slashed at imaginary foes. A shower of apples and oranges fell on the platform. Almost before they touched, they were met by the fell edge of McGonagall's claymore, and cut to pieces. The Bard was beaded with perspiration and orange juice. The audience yelled with delight; McGonagall yelled louder still, and with a fury which I fancy was not wholly feigned.

The cult of McGonagall, the world's worst poet, is the obverse of the cult of Burns, whom many Scotsmen believe to be the world's best, but the result is the same: for to read him – even to be familiar with the titles of some of his poems – is to excuse oneself from reading anyone else. He is now a phenomenally successful joke in the place from which he was banished when he wished to be taken seriously.

★   ★   ★

While I was sitting with my feet up at Gerry Mangan's lodge reading McGonagall's *Poetic Gems* with its wonderful introductory auto-biography ('Well I must say, the first man who ever threw peas at me was a publican . . . '), the news came over the radio that the trains would be going back on the rails forthwith. The union, which had embarked on the strike recklessly after another union's sudden volte-face, had given in.

I was unexcited, though the news ought to have affected me. Travelling in the discomfort of buses had begun to appeal to me, and it was cheaper.

So, for Aberdeen, I boarded once again at the bus station in Dundee. This time I secured a seat on the express without difficulty. The couple next to me on the long seat at the rear had a small baby to whose constant, monotonous girning they were oblivious.

The man in front opened the skylight ventilator, raising the dust from the floor in a small tornado on to my lap.

I closed it.

He opened it.

Outside Dundee, painted in two-foot-high letters on the side of a bridge, we saw the message of the SNP splinter group, Ceartas, echoing the cry of the Glasgow martyrs of 1820:

SCOTLAND FREE OR A DESERT!

Outside Aberdeen, on a sandwich board at the entrance to a filling station:

Remember to check your OIL

4

5,000? 10,000? 20,000?

I

Adrian Blissett, troubleshooter, reached for his wallet and threw it open on the table before me. It was thick with money in various currencies and both flaps were lined with international credit cards.

'Look at that.' It was as if he were seeing it himself for the first time. 'It's impressive, isn't it?' He picked it up, withdrew a note, then folded the wallet and put it away. For a moment he looked disgusted – with the oil business, his part in it, and with Aberdeen.

'People think this business is all glamour, but it isn't, I can tell you, it's bloody hard work too, you know.'

We sat at a low glass table with our drinks. 'What do you want to know? I know *everything* about the oil business.' He had a way of karate-chopping into his own speech when emphasising a word or a phrase. 'You can ask me anything.'

There was nothing in particular I needed to know, no question to which only a troubleshooter could give the answer, though I found myself wishing there was.

'Just to talk about this and that,' I replied inadequately.

'Anything you like.' Chop.

After a pause, I asked, 'What's your job?'

Understandably, he looked disappointed. He was six foot six, wearing a dark-grey suit and handsome from the distance at which I had first seen him on entering the cocktail bar of the hotel. 'You'll recognise me right away,' he had assured me during our telephone conversation earlier in the day. 'I'm six-six and very blond.' Close up, the dark suit made his dull eyes duller.

Contacting him had not been easy. The first time I rang his office, his secretary said he was in London; next time he was in Paris. Three nights a week, normally, he stayed in Aberdeen's most expensive hotel, which drops its prices by half at weekends.

'I don't like this troubleshooter lark. It suggests the TV image, the big money, the girls. It isn't like that – not at all.'

He went on to describe his work in a necessarily sketchy fashion: apart from the flying, which he loved and hated simultaneously, it involved negotiating contracts, keeping the pressure of his workforce high, giving the go-ahead on drilling after the experts had had their say.

He leaned forward in the deeply cushioned chair and, keeping his eyes on his reflection in the table, drew my attention to a group of men standing at the bar. I had noticed them already, by their noisy conversation.

'Don't look up too suddenly. But you see the one in the red shirt with his back to us? Well, that guy is getting it,' the edge of his hand guillotined the table, 'this Friday. He knows it, and he knows that I'm the one who has to tell him – officially.'

'Is he local?'

Adrian Blissett shook his head. I had reminded him of something.

'We're very concerned with the local community,' his voice underwent a shift of register, 'but it's just a fact. Most of the jobs, how can I put it, *available* for locals are of the unskilled sort. You see? It's inevitable. Take someone in my position. I wouldn't have stayed in Aberdeen all my life if I'd happened to be born here. The locals who remain here tend to be of the unskilled sort – the educated ones don't want to stay. You have to *import* people with expertise.'

'Are there no local people in top jobs?'

'Oh, of course. One or two. But when you think about it, they've all had to be brought back to Aberdeen, from down south or abroad. Skill travels well. It's something we're thinking about all the time.'

I had read somewhere of an antagonism between the new Aberdeen, which is oil, and the old Aberdeen, which is fishing.

'Look. Let's not shed crocodile tears over this. Fishing in Aberdeen is in decline, it's as simple as that. The press blame it on the oil industry, but it's *not* the fault of oil – it's the fault of the fishing business itself. Only twenty per cent of last year's salmon catch is expected this year. Twenty per cent! Imagine! There just aren't enough fish in the sea. Anyway, the fishermen I meet – they come to me and complain, looking for sympathy, and then drive away in their Rovers and Porsches. My heart bleeds for them!'

'Possibly the owners,' I said, taken off guard, 'but not your average guy gutting a fish.'

'I'm not talking about the workforce, for God's sake, I'm talking about the *industry*.'

I did not say so, but thought I must have missed a link somewhere. Whatever the links were – between the oil and the fishing industries, between the oil industry and the community, between the oil industry and the Scottish Office, the local council, various departments and boards – they were made from banknotes, which meant that the time for co-operation was limited. Adrian Blissett understood this part of his job well: 'I don't want to co-operate with people, I want to control them.'

He introduced me to the group standing at the bar. There were four of them: one, a large-headed, fatherly-looking man with white hair, Adrian introduced as Henry, 'my right-hand man and I'm his'; two were from other companies; and there was the man in the red shirt whose job had only two days left to live. He was drunk and spoke in a series of jokes and insults intended as jokes. Most of his funny lines were about 'poofters', any mention of which seemed guaranteed to jab the others into raucous laughter. He appeared to hold no grudge against Adrian, his appointed and recognised executioner, and even insisted, in that aggressive fashion which only a Scotsman can achieve, on paying for two extensive rounds of drinks in succession.

Adrian looked dubiously into the bottom of his glass before accepting. Politely, I declined. Another poofter joke; more raucous laughter.

Red shirt touched the back of my hand. 'Don't let it worry you.'

He paid for the drinks with one large note unwrapped from a wad kept in the breast pocket of his shirt, drank his very quickly, then disappeared into the night. One of the others said he had thirty miles to drive to Peterhead.

'He'll never make it.'

'He's made it every night so far.'

'One of these times he won't.'

'I thought he was having it off with . . . ' The one who was speaking glanced discreetly in the direction of reception, where a largish, not unattractive girl was sorting papers behind the desk.

'He *was*.'

'Has he turned queer?'

'He'd need to be to get off with her!' More laughter; more touching.

Adrian's mouth smiled. He detached himself and stood a few feet from the others at the bar. He wanted to talk, he said; it was good for him to talk to someone outside the business. He pushed aside the glass containing the untouched whisky bought for him by the man he would soon be firing. He had to be up early, he said, offering it to me. He worked a twelve-hour day, sometimes longer. He had given up smoking lately and for something to do as we stood in silence for a few moments, cracked his knuckles. One of the two men from the other companies walked across the room towards reception. Without turning round completely and ignoring Adrian, I couldn't make out what the situation was.

'That's another side of the industry you're seeing there.' He winked.

I had heard Aberdeen described as 'Sin City', but so far my walks through its clean and prosperous streets made me wonder where whoever coined the expression had found his material.

Adrian wanted to appear conscientious.

'The local people are always complaining about it, and I don't really blame them. They think their daughters are going wild – this is all so *new* to them. But to be quite frank, I wouldn't lay a local bird.'

'Why not?' It sounded incongruous. But he looked at me as if the answer were posted on the walls.

'I don't want a trip to the clinic – *that's* bloody well why not.'

'Wouldn't a trip to the clinic be as likely in . . . Paris or London?'

He shook his head and patted my arm. 'In those places they're more used to it. Here it's still a novelty. They don't know how to cope with it yet. Girls here, in our office, girls I work beside, their husbands are off-shore for two weeks at a time. What do you think they're doing? They're not sitting at home sewing, are they? Then, when hubby comes home for two weeks, they get a bit of money and they go out and spend it, don't they? They're all at it. It's everywhere.

'Did you see that hotel next door as you came in? Well, when I first came up here, years ago, I went in there and asked for a room for the night and the girl at reception asked if I would like a cup of tea in the morning. So I said yes, that would be very nice, thank you very much. And she said, will it be tea for one or tea for two, sir? I looked at her: I said, just one. And she said, well would you like to *make* it for two, sir?'

He leaned back and folded his arms.

'I'm not going to tell you the end of that story, but that's just another example.'

We were joined by Henry the right-hand man, as the group at the bar finally dispersed. I noticed that the receptionist was still at her desk. She continued sorting with a smile, though I couldn't tell what it was for. The talk between the two men turned to business: other people's salaries, rival companies, clients seen that day and to be seen the next; they talked of 'stimulation concessions', 'depletion curves' and an 'involuting hyperbolic spiral'; the machismo of jargon compounding the master machismo of profit and loss.

'Sorry to talk shop, James.' Adrian Blissett returned to me for a moment as I gathered my things and regretted having to leave. 'But in a way this is really business.'

Troubleshooter faced troubleshooter.

'Isn't it, Henry? How much would you say we had made for our company tonight, just by talking? Five thousand? Ten thousand? Twenty thousand?'

II

Off-shore, on-shore. Multinationals. Choppers, field, rig, derrick and platform. Drilling and diving, welding and weather forecasting and killing a well. Shell, BP, Total, Gulf, Oxy, Conoco, Expro; the Seven Sisters. Houston, Rotterdam, Libya, the Gulf.

These words are not jargon, but part of everyday speech in Aberdeen, of young and old alike, used in counterpoint to complaints about prices in restaurants and estate agencies.

Estimates of the number of oil-related jobs vary, but one puts the figure at 40,000; a multiplication from 3,000 in seven years. In the same period, oil companies have increased from 86 to 750.

It was the Boom. But booms come and go quickly in a country where pessimism is a native faculty. On 12 August 1982, the *Scotsman* published an article by a local journalist which foretold the withering of Aberdeen's oil industry. On 13 August, the same newspaper had a report based on a new Scottish Economic Bulletin, which glowed with 'the sustaining effect of the North Sea oil industry'. The reason for the contradiction, which in a similar form can be found week in, week out, lies not in the ineptitude of journalists, but in the nature of the economy itself.

Scotland, to them, is just another stopping place; just one more element in the infinitely complex calculations of the so-called 'seven sisters', the immensely powerful corporations which run the world's oil industry and to which Aberdeen owes its present fame and fortune. Set these companies' resources against the modest expertise and influence available to bodies like the Grampian Regional Council and it becomes at once apparent that, for all their happy prattling about Aberdeen's long-term future as an oil industry centre, councillors and their officials have no real control over the forces shaping the city's economic destiny. The oilmen are in Aberdeen because it suits them to be there. Some day, sooner or later, it will suit them to depart.

James Hunter, *Scotsman*,
12 August 1982

In pubs, cafés, cinema queues and living rooms, the talk, like most other things, is oil-related. Strangers are assumed to be chasing a piece of the action.

'You'll be up looking for work?' asked the lady in whose house I stayed.

She was the perfect landlady, Mrs Ogilvie. She offered me the choice of two rooms: one of them was spacious, with a desk, overlooking the River Dee, but also a busy main road with a lot of oil-related traffic noise; the other was cramped, without a desk or a view, and silent. I chose the latter. Mrs Ogilvie tutted.

'Young lad like you.'

Every morning at breakfast, she talked of her coming holiday in

the Highlands, where she went every year with her father: six weeks
away; just less than six weeks away; five and a half weeks away . . .

'Have you lived here all your life?'

'Och, goodness, no! Only since 1929.'

'I hope the weather stays fine for your holiday.'

'You used to be able to depend on good weather, but not
nowadays.'

Had it been left up to her, the oil would have stayed where it was,
in the ground, under the sea. She put the blame on the SNP, for
stirring it up.

'I canna be doin' wi' Gordon Wilson. What's he like?'

'He'd make a good Sunday School teacher.'

'I canna be doin' wi' the SNP at a'. How can folk no just be proud
to be British and let that be the end o' it?'

Surely the oil industry had brought a general increase in prosperity
to all Aberdonians?

Mrs Ogilvie and I looked across the river to where the dinosaurs on
wheels were taking their cargo, to the shining turbines and bright
reflecting glass of the new Torry industrial estate. It wasn't that we
were disagreeing, but she saw things differently. She would be
seventy next year, and her father, who lived with her, was over
ninety. He had come from Fife more than half a century ago, to work
in fish-processing. The small factory where he had worked as the
foreman was bought over years ago and now it had gone altogether.
The value of their house, which she and her late husband had bought
for two thousand pounds, had risen to such a figure that ten thousand
added to or subtracted from it would have made no difference to her
appreciation of it as a fortune. But what she was trying to say to me
was that nowadays she seldom left the house after dark.

III

Aberdeen is not a brutal city, but a handsome one, conscious of
appearances. The long, straight main thoroughfare, Union Street, is
presided over not by a commanding castle or a well-bred town hall,
but by the Salvation Army Citadel, a gothic revival building,
attractive in the tantalising manner of such spiralled and turreted

piles. Like almost every important building in the city, it is made from spangled grey granite.

No one referred much to 'The Granite City' in the conversations I had; it was 'the oil town' or 'the boom town'. Comparisons with Houston are easily come by, but Houston was built with the code of expansion in its genes; Aberdeen is a quiet girl at a party who has been asked to sing.

Nonetheless, the rigs and platforms and all the oil-related industries – off-shore, on-shore – are part of the city now. The one which I visited was a hundred and ten miles away in the North Sea.

*   *   *

The chopper whirred monotonously overhead, making conversation uneasy. We waited an unconscionably long time on the sidelines while the pilot hung on for a sea mist to clear. Eventually, we boarded. The interior of the helicopter was unexpectedly cramped: roughly twelve seats, all except mine and that of the girl from the Petroleum Company occupied by rig workers returning after their on-shore leave, which might have lasted seven, fourteen or twenty-eight days.

There was a period around 1974–5 when some of my friends went to work in the North Sea. It was a kind of El Dorado with black gold. The work was acknowledged to be hard, but equally the pay was said to be good. The former, however, always seemed to outweigh the latter, and these refugees from unfinished college courses or the labour exchange never stuck it for very long.

Inside the chopper there was a ritual which, like everything else about the flight, was a condensed version of what happens in an aeroplane. I fastened my seat belt, fastened my life belt, and tried to concentrate on the instructions for inflating it – patently infeasible, it seemed, in the straits which would demand the action, although six months later a chopper bound for the same platform came down in the sea, and all seventeen on board were rescued. I adjusted the band inside my yellow hard hat, and politely declined the earplugs offered by Petroleum's girl, Moira.

'You'll be deafened.'

'It'll be good experience.'

Choppers fly low. The land below was seen in sections, green, brown, yellow, grey, very close, which made the sensation of flying more urgent than usual. From the sky, the oil platform seemed remarkably compact: a top-heavy, clumsy affair, all scaffolding, with two giant flares for burning off excess gas in order to avoid heat damage to the platform. They were situated at the corners, like guns on a lookout post, perpetually shooting twenty-foot lengths of flame into the atmosphere.

We landed on a broad square of green, marked H.

The Installations Manager was called Matt: a portly, fidgety Oklahoman. He had fine leather, decorated cowboy boots on his feet and, wrapped around his wrist, a broad watchstrap studded with glass or jewels, with which the other hand played continually.

He was going to be frank. On this platform they had experience of the press (his index finger polished something emerald-coloured on the other wrist); he admired them a lot, sometimes, and appreciated that they had a valuable job to do.

'But.' The hand came off the watchstrap and pointed at me. 'And this is nothing personal against you – we're glad to have you here, the Company is glad to have you here.' Moira, who worked on-shore in public relations, nodded in agreement. 'But . . . in my experience, sometimes the press only wants to talk about money. Now, that's not *all* the Company does out here, is make money.' He laughed, and gave me time to laugh as well, keeping his eyes on me. 'Don't be offended now. I said I was going to be frank.'

I wasn't offended.

'So-o . . . '

So. He wished to talk about anything, except money. He promised to show me the workings of the platform, later on. First, he told me about his twelve-year-old daughter, her horse, his wife, their cars, the house which they had had built specially, the affection which daughter, wife and himself all shared for Aberdeen and how easily they had fitted into the local community.

'That's very important where I come from, the community. When I'm on-shore during leave, all I do is relax. Go bowling, driving . . . relax. The telephone in our house rings all the time, but it's never for me, always my wife and daughter. That's just the way I like it. I never want the telephone to ring for me. If it's for me, it means there is trouble in *here*.' He pointed to the floor.

How did he like life on the rigs?

'Well, you see, out here, the Company makes a point of seeing that the food is good. My wife – '

'And the men?'

'The men like it. They *seem* to like it anyway.' He laughed. 'If they're still here in the morning I figure they like it enough, and my work's done. But we make a special point of looking after a man's stomach out here. If his stomach's okay the rest of him's gonna be okay.'

'The food *is* good,' Moira confirmed. She was thinking of the wives.

'What's your job?' I asked Matt.

'My job? Well, if everything's running smoothly, I figure I don't have no job!' He laughed loudly and rimmed the jewels. It was a line I was to hear repeated often throughout the afternoon. I was about to ask if I might go and speak to some of the men – in this windowless little room I wasn't getting very far – when Matt put his cowboy boots on the desk and began to explain the rhythm of the day's work to me. Continuous production meant a working day – and a workforce – divided into two twelve-hour shifts. On this platform, most but not all of the men worked a seven-day-on, seven-day-off shift, which he said was the most popular.

'Are many of them local?'

'Half and half, I'd say.'

And management: the deputy Installations Manager, for example?

'He's the same as me. Same state, in fact – state of Oklahoma. My wife and his wife . . . '

I tried a different approach. He'd said he never wanted to hear the telephone ring at home: was there an occasion when it *had* rung?

Yes, there was.

Could he tell me why.

Well . . .

Before he could change the subject again, Moira piped up:

'The extortionist, Matt?'

Matt bit his lip.

'You had an extortionist?'

'Oh yes.' Moira remembered the situation, and the panic it had bred, as if it had been yesterday.

'Really, the whole operation, on-shore and on the rigs, was just one *big* panic.'

A former worker had posted notes to Matt composed of letters snipped from newspapers, informing him that the platform had been fitted up with dynamite, and suggesting a reward to himself for not blowing it up. The first message gave a warning and the second made a threat.

'How did you know he was a former worker?'

'By his knowledge of the installations.'

'How much money?'

'Uh, a lot,' said Matt.

'A hundred thousand pounds,' said Moira.

A lot, but less, as I was to discover later, than the value of the oil produced in one hour on this platform.

'What happened?'

'Oh, we gottim.'

'The police knew he was an ex-worker,' Moira explained, 'but there were too many ex-workers to track down and make checks on in the time available. So the money was got ready and we asked the person where it should be left. He gave directions for the exact placing, and said in his next letter that it was to be put inside a trash can.'

'That was his big mistake,' Matt took it up. 'Only Americans say "trash can", see? We got him after that.'

Matt was looking jumpy; on that occasion he had had a job to do. He stood up, very tall in his cowboy boots.

'Come and have some lunch before the kitchen closes. You must be hungry.'

'You'll find the food's *very* good,' said Moira, and glanced at my notebook to check if I had written it down.

Moving from place to place on an oil platform is like playing a giant game of snakes and ladders, with oneself as the counter. To walk from one side to the other would take less than a minute, but walking straight is impossible where the utilisation of space is vertically, and not horizontally, engineered. Most of the workers complain of confinement – seeing the same faces, the same environment, day after day, night after night. It's like being on a ship that doesn't move. There is no alcohol, since it would be easy for a Scotsman to fall off a platform into the sea, and no sex, or at least no women.

Moira was enjoying the looks and suggestions which followed us everywhere. The last time a woman had walked on this platform had been a month ago, and the woman was Moira. On that occasion she had escorted a television crew who wanted to make a film about life in the North Sea.

'All they wanted to talk about was money, money, money,' said Moira. 'So I gave them the brush-off in the end.'

My guided tour ended in the control room, the largest on the platform, which allows more space for the pin-ups that decorate every wall. About ten men were working at floor-to-ceiling panels of buttons and glass screens showing needles and flashing digits. Our arrival was expected and a kettle had been boiled to make coffee. However, since our entrance coincided with an emergency, we never got it.

Without any apparent reason, the oil had stopped flowing.

The oil had stopped flowing!

The reaction was one of daze rather than of panic. Men stood at different panels, caught in various postures of impotence. A lot of energy went into pressing what seemed to be random combinations of buttons. Instructions cross-fired the length and breadth of the room. Two men bumped into each other on their way to reach a single control button which related to a digital clock. One of them pressed it but the effect on the red figures was nil. Still no oil.

A panel was opened up, and then another one, and screwdrivers were applied to the innards. One man in a dark-blue overall whose position of authority was unclear began to panic more than the others. The more he was ignored, the louder he shouted. Although no one seemed willing to shut him up, his contribution to the scene was merely to increase confusion.

He was bawling at a man with a screwdriver when Matt placed his hand on his shoulder and said something into his ear. Then he approached the corner where I was standing, sucking his lower lip. Perhaps I had better follow him downstairs . . . Moira would be happy to make me a cup of coffee in his office . . .

His attention was distracted by a man in a yellow hard hat asking for advice about a set of buttons, and he turned his back on me.

Twenty minutes later, the oil started to flow once more. A blockage of some form, one of the men explained; nothing dangerous, as it turned out, but alarming all the same, and costly. There was some nervous sniggering around the room when 'our American friends' were mentioned.

'How much was lost?'

'A lot?'

'Roughly, how much?'

A quick computation was made: 4,000 barrels, at $35 a barrel: $140,000.

'Our American friends won't be pleased to hear about it.' He glanced at Moira. 'If they ever do.'

Matt ushered me upstairs again, unruffled.

'You see, that's when I have a job to do. Like I say, if everything's running smoothly, I don't have no job. If the telephone rings . . . '

One or two people stopped and questioned him on our way back to the office, and he calmly smoothed feathers and handed out assurances.

On the way back to the helicopter, we passed through the recreation room, where it seemed the entire population of the platform was slouched before the television, sleeping or else lethargically wishing away the hours to the next period of leave, and a renewed acquaintance with beer, fish and chips and women's voices. Round the pool table, a foursome played silently, looking up in unison when Moira passed. A particularly salacious pin-up caught my eye, as it had done on the way in. Beside it was a hand-written note, which read:

If you have a HEART then please return the two gold rings which were taken from CABIN 13 last Thursday. GREAT sentimental value.

Eyes sought to discern Moira's figure beneath the heavy clothing she had donned to protect herself against the strong wind as we dashed towards the helicopter across the green landing strip.

IV

Eventually, I happened on Sin City, quite by accident, and found it more my kind of place, though only just, than the expensive cocktail bar of one of Aberdeen's pseudo-elegant hotels.

It was a grimy pub on the wharf. To reach it, I had to pass along the dockside, over rusty, disused rails and massive chains drooping from capstans into the water. Fishing boats shared the dock with tugs and service ships.

The first few pubs I tested were dull places, with westerns on video, or a Country & Western singer crooning in the corner. In this boom town, some of them had signs saying 'No facilities for women'. It was my last night in Aberdeen and I felt like company and conversation. Prowling the streets was tiring, as was sitting around waiting for return calls at Mrs Ogilvie's house. A simple chat, about football or the Falklands, never seemed more desirable.

The Waterloo Bar, then, attracted me because it looked as if it had some life in it; indeed, from outside it sounded like the scene of a wrestling match. It was small, with an L-shaped bar, and full of drunks – not such a common sight inside a Scottish pub as might at first be thought, since a law prohibits the sale of alcohol to anyone already under the influence. But this was the land of inhibition.

The barman, a chap in his thirties with a large head and hands, was deaf and dumb. I asked for a bottle of Guinness and he nodded and began to pour a pint of lager. With difficulty, I regained his attention and stated my order again. He raised a finger in a gesture of comprehension, smiled his apology, and started pouring a *half* pint of lager. At the third attempt we got it, which wasn't bad under the circumstances. I sipped the sour stout and looked around: most other customers were drinking pints of lager.

The men were oil workers, attached to service vessels, most of them in dirty clothes. It was hard to tell who had finished work, who was just beginning, and who had skipped out for a fly drink.

A squat, bullet-headed Dutchman with eyes like slate staggered from place to place, deliberately crowding people who were ordering drinks from the bar or having a conversation. Occasionally, he would stop in front of someone and try to stare him out –

which seemed difficult for him to do. No one was irked or bored enough to want a fight.

A line of women sat on stools at the horseshoe bar, their space apparently reserved. The farthest from me was very large and gingerbread coloured with conspicuous freckles. She drank vodka lazily and conversed across the floor with the quieter-looking men posted along the walls. Next to her sat an even larger woman with rats' tails hair and an absurd, party-sweet egg-blue dress which had been tortured into containing her. Beside her was a petite black girl in a red ra-ra skirt with white spots. She looked girlish and desirable when she sang along to the loud jukebox sounds, clapping her hands on thin, bare thighs. When the music stopped she barked insults at men in a Geordie accent, until the next record came on.

A few feet away, another pair were involved in separate discussion. One had suffered sixty years in twenty, while the other was blonde and pretty in the office-secretary style, and was getting attention from several drunk men. One of them put his arms around her and clung to her back and pawed her from behind as she gave serious advice to her friend; she took no notice when his hands cupped and squeezed her breasts and his cheek rubbed against her hair like a cat rubbing itself on a window pane. She continued talking to her friend, pausing only to light a cigarette, appearing not to notice even when his fingers clumsily undid a button on her white blouse and disappeared inside.

In this room were all the scabs and bruises of oil-related life, pressed together into a single hardness, every excuse for displays of emotion having been squeezed out. Only a tattooed lady looking out from someone's open-necked shirt or 'Mother' on a forearm or a primitive command to follow – as with the pin-ups which covered the walls of the platform – spoke of a deeper need.

The Dutchman made another inelegant tour of the room and landed at the shoulder of the fat gingerbread lady. He tried to kiss her, almost fell over, and was saved only by her hand raised to push him away. But then she stood up, said something to her friends, and they left together.

The jukebox music brought looks of lovely suggestiveness to the close-cropped black girl's face as she sang.

Ive been undressed by kings and Ive seen some things . . .

The blonde continued to counsel her shrivelled friend. It was a terribly serious problem they were discussing, and the friend's black eye kept it that way.

'. . . . . .'

'. . .'

The stubby fingers of the man clinging to her back fondled her while she gazed at her companion with pity and shook her head in sympathy.

5

The Captive Tongue

The car pushed north, through Huntly, Keith and Elgin, into Highland territory. It was after three o'clock and I had not eaten since breakfast at half past seven in the morning, but I was growing accustomed to the irregular life. The towns and villages we dipped into were dull, flattered by sunshine; however, a motorist's eye-view should not be trusted.

Angus Duff was surprised to discover that I had had no lunch, and insisted on pulling in at the next roadside café. It was a place which bragged about its newness, with an artificial log-cabin front and a sign at the door proclaiming 'Fast Food'. Inside, lounge music oozed from loudspeakers placed strategically round the room, which made it impossible to avoid the sound. The waitress stood before us bedecked with tartan bunting which disguised her pretty looks. I ordered a cup of tea and a sandwich, and Angus asked for beer. She disappeared without a word or a sign of having absorbed our requests, then returned a few minutes later with a salad sandwich made from white sliced bread, the crusts politely trimmed.

I had not seen Angus Duff for fifteen years, until we met by accident in Aberdeen. As boys, we were friends in his home village of Portmahomack, where I arrived most summers to spend my annual holidays, staying on a farm without television or telephone, where the water pump in the yard continued in use until the late 1950s, and remnants of the Gaelic tongue floated on the air. In the bay, close to the shore, Angus and I used to fish from his father's boat. A good day for me was one when his catch was no more than six times greater than mine. In spite of every effort, on both our parts, his 'secret' was found to be untransmittable.

Portmahomack is situated near the northern tip of the heel which projects into the North Sea above the Black Isle and ends in the beacon of Tarbat Ness. A small village, its staple industries were once linen, grain and fishing, with the emphasis on fishing. Last century, the village population doubled during the proper season, as about two hundred boats arrived with crews eager to prosper by helping in the herring curing. In mid-century, Portmahomack had one hundred and twelve vessels using its harbour (improved by Thomas Telford) every year.

Until a few years ago, fishing remained an important factor in the local economy and several small boats used to leave the pier twice each day. Now, here as elsewhere in the North, fishing has deteriorated – 'There's nothing down there,' Angus said – and latest improvements in the village are not to the harbour (though it is badly in need of them) but to the promenade and other facilities for the increasing number of holidaymakers who come to the Port every summer. Men who once were fishermen nowadays work at Nigg, where Europe's largest yard for the construction of oil platforms was opened in 1972.

Angus too was employed at Nigg, and had been in Aberdeen only to attend a meeting. He said he would be returning to Port-mahomack next day and why didn't I join him. After some reluctance, I agreed to do so. My target was Sutherland, but after nights of strange beds, the thought of seeing some familiar faces for a day or two was comforting, and I wondered aloud why I hadn't suggested it myself. Perhaps going back after years away made me more uneasy than I cared to admit, with the nervousness that comes from visiting a former lover.

I finished my sandwich, tried to pay the waitress, who pointed dumbly at the cash register on the desk, and then we stepped outside again into the sunshine, where Angus's Triumph was waiting. He turned the key in the ignition and the radio came on automatically, releasing the mid-Atlantic babble of a Radio Highland DJ into the sweaty saloon.

With the windows open, we flew past signs for Alness, Cromarty, Invergordon, Tain . . . Glad of the excuse provided by the radio not to talk for a while, I enjoyed the sense of entering another country.

Early travellers called the Highlands '*La sauvage Ecosse*' and returned to the safer south with tales of half-clad, strange-tongued barbarians, hard black stones which burned and trees sprouting geese which, when they landed on the ground, turned to stone, but on falling into the sea assumed life and flew into the air.

During the sixteenth and seventeenth centuries, Highlanders were called, with contempt, 'Irish'. One traveller of 1689 warned, 'Too many retain not only the Irish language, but the Irish religion.'

That is less the case now, as a result of the brutal fervour with which the government put out the embers of the Forty-five Rising after the Battle of Culloden in 1746. The savage aftermath was aimed at eradicating 'the Irish language' and much else besides. A series of acts rushed through Parliament following the Hanoverian victory were meant to emasculate the Gael who survived it. Arms were forbidden, understandably, by the Disarmament Act, which also regarded the bagpipes as a weapon of war and banned them as well. More unusual, and humiliating, was the Disclothing Act, which forbade the wearing of Highland Dress: 'that is to say, the Philabeg, or Little Kilt, Trowse, Shoulder-Belts or any Part whatsoever of what peculiarly belongs to the Highland Garb.'

It is a harsh and absurd law which prevents a man putting on his clothes, but they meant it: anyone caught wearing the kilt was liable to be transported to 'any of His Majesty's plantations beyond the seas'.

Although it is often said that the Act was ignored in many places, even unenforcable, the campaign of which it was a part achieved its objective at last, at least in some measure, for the kilt is a bit of a joke today, even in the Highlands, and Gaelic is spoken mainly by peasant people, or enthusiasts.

Above the pop music, Angus continued to answer my questions about the village.

'Donald Ross? He's off somewhere – down south, I think, I couldn't tell you exactly where. Donald Sutherland, he's away too. No, not England – to Canada.'

'What about Donald the minister's son?'

'Oh, Donald Duff! Poor Donald, I haven't heard of him for a long time. He got all mixed up with a bad crowd.'

'You mean hard drinkers?'

'No, no, the wrong kind of things – drugs and all that.'

There were others who had not moved away, and their story was similar to that of most people who spend whole lifetimes in small places: a few were prospering, most were the same; a shopkeeper might have died and his son be running down the business; a girl I knew from our early teens was still unmarried but had had a baby . . . Angus was pretty certain he could tell me who the father was. And then there were others who had thought the unthinkable, given up their city lives and the potential fortunes promised by them, and returned home – to work at Nigg, which is within commuting distance of Portmahomack. It was a different kind of prosperity now from that which came with fishing.

'You used to have a baker's shop, a butcher's shop, a draper's shop in the Port. Now you have nothing. And yet there are more people there than before. It's strange, isn't it?'

As we approached the village, Angus told me of the latest attempt to buy the land on which Portmahomack sits, and turn the whole place into a summer resort – 'something glittery', Angus said. The Grenair Company, a consortium based in Bedford, who had owned it, had gone into liquidation, to the general relief of the local people. But there was still some unease about the intentions of the new owners, compounded by dissatisfaction with the way in which the Bedford company had concentrated on the 'glitter' to the detriment of traditionally essential features, like the harbour which had a gaping hole in it.

'They build you chalets at the drop of a hat,' said Angus without rancour, 'but you can't get them to lay out a few quid on patching up the harbour.'

He left me at the village boundary, in view of the sign at the caravan park which still forbade the entrance or exit of vehicles on a Sunday, and I walked down the crescent-shaped main street which has the sea and sand on one side and houses in many colours on the other. It is the most colourful, the least enclosed, the least ashamed, the most joyful, of all Highland villages (in spite of being served by the Free Church) and possesses a cosmopolitanism which is not the return from black gold, but the legacy of those two hundred boats which used to come every year for the herring curing, depositing their crews from places far and wide. This contact between villagers and outsiders may illuminate the complaint made in the first *Statistical Account of Scotland* of 1792, which scolds at the 'droves' of young people who go south and 'never return'.

The first familiar face I saw belonged to Joe, a retired worker from the farm we used to stay on when I was a child. He greeted me with a friendly hand, and then began to talk in a way that made me realise he had mistaken me for my father. He continued to do so even when I had corrected him.

'My, but you're looking well!' He shook his head in amazement at my father's youthfulness and enquired about the children. Then, like Angus – like most people you meet in familiar villages – began telling me who was living here and who was not.

'Donald Mackay? He's working at Nigg – '

A red sports car came to a sudden halt beside us where we stood in Harbour Street and an elderly man leaned out of the window, exchanged a few words with Joe, gave a curt hello to me, then took off quickly again. I said something about the number of holiday-makers in the village, and Joe regarded me oddly.

'I thought you would know him, Harry – Big Jim Chisolm. Retired now, like; but used to have the fishing boat you and your laddie were so fond of.'

II

To reach Finlay Ross's house next day, I first had to walk a mile to the village of Rockfield, which is on the other side of the heel – the *tarbat* – from Portmahomack. At supper time, Angus and his wife had confirmed the rumour of Highland hospitality, and it made the road hard going. It was eight o'clock and warm. This far north at least another three hours of good light could be expected, maybe more. Each change in the position of the setting sun arranged the seascape and the clouds banked on the horizon differently. To the south were neatly apportioned fields, to the east the sand and the sea, to the north yellow flowers of the whin braes.

I walked downhill into Rockfield, a tiny village huddled in the shelter of Rockfield Cliffs, to the accompaniment of a shrill chorus of gulls. The sea on this side of the tarbat was, if anything, even more still, more green. Rockfield seemed to presume no reason why anyone should know or care of its existence, and to be quite content with that result. It had neither shop nor pub nor any other public facility except a telephone box, which stood conspicuously in the middle of its only street.

Scarcely any fishing goes on in Rockfield, as in Portmahomack. Flat on the ground on the rocky shore lay a batch of poles which I remembered used to be erected for drying fishing nets. One or two private boats sat upturned, like giant turtles, on the grassy flat which fronted the rocks. Almost every house had its front door wide open, but I passed no one on my way through except a couple of dogs and a man polishing his car, who called out to me in a cheerful voice.

Finlay, now thirty-eight, has left the district only to make necessary visits – weddings, funerals – to Glasgow or Edinburgh. He moved house for the first and only time seven years ago when he married a local girl. They set up home near Rockfield and Finlay left his mother in the Port, although he visited her every day. He is a big man with fair, curly hair and blue eyes. Before learning the trade of welder fairly late in life, he worked as a tractor driver and odd-job man on various farms.

They have a daughter who looks like her mother, Tina Duff (Highland women traditionally keep their own names), and she looks like her mother and her mother's mother. I know this even though I have never met Finlay's mother-in-law, for Katy, like her mother Tina, has a stern resistance in her lips and eyes which may reward you with laughter at the proper moment, a look taken from generations of Highland women. It is written that in the time of the Clearances, it was the women who were in the vanguard of the fight against the factors and policemen, whose brutality earned them the nickname of 'the Russians of Ross-shire', and left several women with serious head injuries.

Finlay, Katy and Tina live in a comparatively spacious nineteenth-century house on a hill, overlooking the sea on both sides of the tarbat. Its interior has been completely altered, the original proportions and designs demolished. Finlay himself knocked down walls and took out fireplaces which he replaced with decorated alcoves filled with bric-à-brac. He also covered the old front with cladding stone and replaced the original windows.

'It's a lot of work,' I said.

'It's a lot of work all right – especially just to leave it all behind you.'

'You're leaving?'

'Ach well,' he stood up and refilled my glass before kneeling to top up his own, 'I've been thinking about it. It's been on my mind for a long time now, to tell you the truth.'

Something in his voice forewarned me of the uneasiness this subject would cause. For the first time since we had been reunited, he was talking without the utter confidence I associated with him.

'Where would you go?'

He must have guessed, from my tone, that I was seeking some kind of reassurance, for he raised a large hand and a ripple of laughter ran through his voice.

'Not down there – to the big smoke. I lose my way when I step off the train in London, don't I, Tina? No, to be honest with you I fancy going abroad.'

'Where?'

'I don't know.' He shook his head slowly. He had never been abroad. 'I fancy Norway.'

'Why Norway?'

'I don't know. I just do.'

Tina stood up and left the room, warning the child who sat at our feet that it was almost bedtime. Finlay fiddled with the long neck of the whisky bottle, screwing and unscrewing the cap. I tried to look as if I hadn't noticed the turn in the atmosphere.

Throughout our conversation, little Katy had been watching a bad American comedy on television: it had a black child actor who played the well-liked stooge in a society otherwise made up of whites. They seemed to adore him for his stupidity. For a reason I could not understand, his screen parents were also white.

The large colour set had a video recorder plugged into it, presently lying dormant beneath the television table. Finlay had bought it from a shop in Tain. When I first arrived, I had noticed a collection of taped movies, spines arranged like books along a shelf, in one of the alcoves. In another corner, a complicated stereo system crouched silently on the floor, its two speakers snuggling together. It looked as if it was sulking, having been usurped by the newly arrived video.

'That bloody thing's out of order,' Finlay said to break the silence. 'I keep forgetting to get it fixed.'

Every so often, the canned laughter from the television distracted him, and he let his concentration wander from me to the screen and back again.

'Ach, but anyway,' he went on, unable to let go of the subject of work, 'Nigg will be good for another few years yet. Or so they say. I'll be quite honest with you, I make more money there in a month than I used to make in half a year up the road on one of the farms.' He pursed his lips and looked business-like.

With that, he suggested a trip to the village for a drink, and I readily accepted. Finlay kissed his daughter and tried to speak to her, but, engrossed in the comedy programme, she wouldn't answer.

'Katy, say goodnight to Daddy.'

'Shhh,' said Katy.

Finlay turned to me and raised his eyebrows to the ceiling. Then he tried another method, which did the trick.

'An blaran ach-na-tual shin ba larreich na chalich kil.'

This set Katy into uproarious laughter, and she replied:

'Suig na loan dhu na cladich ach na chanter traigheal' – followed by even greater laughter.

'That's the Gaelic,' said Finlay, addressing me.

For a moment I was taken in. 'You speak Gaelic?'

'No-oo.' He laughed and looked a touch embarrassed at having hoodwinked a guest, even one so credulous. 'Say goodnight again in Gaelic, Katy.'

Katy opened her mouth and another stream of meaningless babble poured out. She was reduced to uncontrollable laughter by the time we left.

'Now she'll never get to sleep,' said Finlay, climbing into his car. I would rather have walked. The sun was blazing down on the rim of the Dornoch Firth. We drove into the village and parked the car before the hotel bar. Finlay applied the key to the driver's door and told me how to lock mine.

'Never had to lock a car door in my life before.'

'That's just what I was thinking.'

'Aye, but lots of people come into the Port now, you see. Oil workers and so on. They're just looking for drink and they get up to all sorts of mischief. The other night John Willie had his car broken into, and a week or two ago four boats was set loose in the harbour. Bloody idiots!'

Inside the recently modernised pub there was a small celebration in progress for a youth recently returned from the Falklands.

I ordered the drinks and after greeting everyone he knew – which was almost everyone in the pub – Finlay returned to our earlier conversation, in a low voice.

'As you could see, it's a touchy subject at the moment. You can imagine why. Not just leaving here and all the family, but I would have to be gone for a few months by myself, to try and find a place for us to live and all that. And then there's the question of a foreign school for Katy. That's if I could *get* a job abroad.'

'Wouldn't you be better off staying at Nigg?' But I was instantly sorry for my unhelpful response. It was exactly the kind of remark he did not want to hear from me. Until the subject changed itself naturally in the course of the conversation, then, I let him do most of the talking and tried to decide if his plans were realistic or not. I myself would not choose to live all my life in a village the size of Portmahomack, no matter how great its charm, yet with Finlay it was different. He had real roots here, which could be too deep to unearth.

The more he talked the more I thought it probable that that was all he would ever do. He was so settled that his security acted as a clamp. There would never be a break from it unless someone else made it for him. Though the community no longer satisfied him, he would only gaze at adventure through symbols of a new world which, ultimately, were more constricting than anything it was within his power to reject.

The talk was broken up, eventually, when Angus arrived in company with his father, whom I had not seen for years. We shook hands and there followed a light-hearted squabble over who was to be allowed to pay for the round of drinks, in which Finlay triumphed.

'Richest man in Ross-shire,' joked Angus's father. In his spare time he was a lobster fisherman and, remembering my boyish enthusiasms, invited me to join him at high tide next day to take the boat and draw in his creels. Gladly, I accepted.

6

Stories in Stones

I

The Gaelic language is generally spoken by the lower class of people throughout the greater part of the parish, but it has certainly lost ground during the last forty years, and, in proportion as the improved system of education advances, it will no doubt continue to advance still more. In proof of this, the presbytery of Caithness have lately come to the decision to discontinue the preaching of the Gaelic language in the eastern district of the parish . . .

The English has not only made encroachments upon the Gaelic territory, but has extended itself over the whole neighbouring district; and indeed were it not that its progress was considerably impeded by the importation of several colonies of Highlanders from the heights of Kildonan and other parts of Sutherland about twenty years ago, when the sheep system commenced there, its triumphs, ere now, would have been still more extensive.

Rev. George Davidson, report on the Parish of Latheron,
including Badbea (1840),
New Statistical Account for Scotland

★ ★ ★

A small set of statistics I came across in a book prompted me to stop for a night at Helmsdale, described in the guide book I carried in a single phrase as 'a grey fishing town'.

In 1811 the Strath of Kildonan, which bends north-westwards from the town, had sixteen hundred inhabitants; a few years later there were just over two hundred. In the same period the population of the parish of Loth – which at the time included Helmsdale – doubled in size.

In the time taken to walk from one end of the Strath of Kildonan to the other, farmers became herring-fishers, their new occupation as decreed by the House of Sutherland. They carried with them what possessions it had been possible to salvage from their cottages before they were set alight by the evicting officers, and drove their animals before them.

The land throughout the Highlands and Islands is littered with the remains of cottages, longhouses and barns. Visitors see clusters of stones, sometimes piled in conical shapes, and ground-markings which at first seem unintelligible, or else are mistaken for pre-historic remains of the type in which the county of Sutherland is particularly rich; seldom do they realise that what they are looking at is the skeleton of a township destroyed during what is known universally as the Highland Clearances, but is hereabouts still called 'the evictions'.

The train north from Tain to Helmsdale swerves to admit the Dornoch Firth, then burrows a way through the high purple mountains of the east coast, passing through Ardgay, Culrain, Invershin; at Lairg it turns right and veers slightly to the south again, tracking the River Fleet which furrows the strath of the same name, halting at Golspie before heading due north once more along the coast.

A journey which is ten miles as the crow flies – from Tain to Golspie – has taken more than one hour, and fifty miles of railway track; but not a single passenger on the train would have objected had it taken four times that length of time. Except those who had travelled on the train before, no one had ever seen rivers and mountains like this.

I anticipated this part of my journey with more excitement than any other, for the simple reason that I believed Sutherland to be the most beautiful of all Scottish counties, and also for the more complex reason that it is perhaps the most melancholy.

The train arrived exactly at noon. I checked into the Bridge Hotel, a large, important-looking building in the heart of the valley where the town of Helmsdale is seated. Established in 1816 as part of the general 'improvements' of the time, which aimed to turn Helmsdale into a major fishing town, the Bridge was one of the few respectable inns in Sutherland at the beginning of the last century.

It was more or less empty, my only fellow guests being a few sportsmen. One of them was attempting to share with the receptionist an enthusiasm for his current reading matter, a book giving details of the arrival in Sutherland of spaceships. She listened patiently, as I queued behind him, a perfect receptionist's smile on her lips.

'This fellow reckons they came from another planet,' the man said.

'Oh yes?' Her voice fairly sang with politeness.

'During pre-history, of course.'

'Uh-huh.'

A note of laughter entered his voice as he suddenly realised how he was appearing to her. He hammered his forehead with the heel of his hand.

'What's the man's name now, I've forgotten. . . . But it would explain a lot about these cairns and brochs and so on that's still such a mystery, wouldn't it?'

'Did they stay long?'

He looked at her. 'I don't know, long enough to make an impression anyway. Standing stones, that's the kind of thing they were interested in. I'll lend you the book if you want. Will you be here tonight?'

She smiled but let him know that she had plenty to keep her busy in the evenings, and turned her attention to the gentleman behind.

I settled my things into the small room to which she led me on the first floor. The corridors of the hotel were long and silent. I went downstairs after a short rest to look for a drink and some lunch, but avoided the bar of the hotel in case I should be forced to listen to more cosmic research on standing stones.

I found a pub near the harbour and went inside; there were no other customers. My first impression of the barman, who was tall and silver-haired, was that he was an English gentleman, but when he spoke I realised how faulty my power of detection could be.

'What brings you here?' he said with a strongly musical Highland accent. Bored with hearing my usual answer, I replied:

'I'm writing something.'

'About Helmsdale?' He seemed to find the idea funny.

'I'm interested in the Highland Clearances.'

'Oh, *that*.' He picked up a glass, twisted it round the towel on his other hand, then held it up to the light. I was afraid of having mentioned a subject which was either too sensitive, or too boring, for him to talk about. Then he suggested a trip to Badbea. I had to ask him to repeat the name.

'You pronounce it *bad*-bay. It's just a village – well, it's only ruins now. It's quite interesting if you like history and that. It's only six miles north of here, across the county border into Caithness. You know the Ousdale Burn?'

He went on with his story, what there was of it; there wasn't much to tell, he said, though he must have known as much as anyone.

'I'm one of them, you see. My grandfather left it as it is now.'

★　★　★

Hardly anything is known about the people who lived on the cliffs at Badbea until this century. No books or pamphlets, so far as I could discover, exist to describe them. They left little behind: a small monument to their own folk, a snapshot of Scotland's history.

In 1813 about eighty people, Polsons, Gunns and Sutherlands, in eleven or twelve families out of thousands evicted from the Strath of Kildonan, came to live here. In the strath, they had survived mainly by farming and by distilling whisky, an illicit occupation which violated the excise laws but carried the blessing of centuries. However, their landlady, the Countess of Sutherland, Marchioness of Stafford and 1st Duchess of Sutherland, demurred; in a letter she commented on the 'refractory' nature of the people of Clan Gunn who were 'unwilling to quit that occupation for a life of industry of a different sort which was proposed to them'.

After some resistance on the part of the people, the policemen employed to carry out the evictions were reinforced by a column of the 21st Foot regiment, which happened to be stationed at nearby Fort George. They arrived with guns.

At Badbea it is not 'unspoiled' – that most insensitive of all epithets applied to the Highlands – it is not even picturesque. The cliffs drop a hundred feet to the sea, and the houses built by the ex-farmers from local stone are perched on a slope which induces vertigo thirty yards from the edge where it meets the sea. The Badbea cattle and children all had to be tethered to prevent them falling down the cliff. The land is resourceless. The houses were built to take a permanent beating from sea winds which are strong and cold even in the summer months.

At the turn of the century, their leader was a man called John Badbea. He owned the only watch in the village and acted as doctor and preacher, delivering his sermons in the Gaelic which, half a century before, as witness the report in the *New Statistical Account*, the presbytery of Caithness had 'come to the decision to discontinue'.

John and his fellow inhabitants fished in the sea below the cliffs, an occupation which in such conditions appears to the untrained eye to be impossible. They also worked on the estate which owned the land they lived on, building dry-stone dykes at the rate of a shilling a day.

The dykes have survived a century and a half of Caithness weather better than the houses; they run for mile after mile without apparent logic. The cottages, though similar in design to those which their occupants left behind in the devastated townships up the strath, have a younger, less mouldered appearance. On some, gables and walls with narrow windows which could be easily blocked up against the perpetual wind, still stand on plentiful ferns, while others are reduced to the familiar pile of stones.

John Badbea emigrated to New Zealand, where he died. In 1911, John Gunn, the last tenant, followed, leaving behind a monument made from the stones of Badbea's house.

Instead of going to the road to wait for a lift back to Helmsdale, I started out with the intention of walking by a direct route along the cliffs. It was going to be difficult. The land was uneven, and the ferns which hid the tussocks I stumbled over also concealed the burn which soaked both my feet. After what seemed like a long way, I came to a track which carried me along comfortably for over a mile. I imagined it might eventually lead back to the town, skipping the ravines of the Ord of Caithness which were visible on the map as cracked black lines, and on the faraway hills as deep folds plunging into the earth.

I came in sight of some more ruined cottages and started towards them, but I got only a few yards before realising that they were the cottages of Badbea. My ancient path, which I had trusted to lead me through the ravines in the footsteps of John Gunn and John Badbea, had only led me round in a circle.

On the way back to the road where I could hitch a lift, I passed another dilapidated cottage, and as I approached to look inside, something small and fleet crossed my path and disappeared behind some rocks, allowing about two seconds' view of its bushy tail. I had disturbed it in the act of devouring a small rabbit, whose torn sinews and reddened bones I found where they had been taken by the wildcat, just inside the entrance to the house.

II

Scotland is an invisible country in the eyes of many. If strangers do not mistake it for a northerly region of England, they are likely to be acquainted only with rumours, such as the beauty of the Highlands. About this rumour there always hangs a suggestion that an 'old life', and hence a better life, survives in the Highlands which today is one of Europe's least populated areas. 'The last great European wilderness' is a definition beloved of seasonal sportsmen, who arrive with the sole intention of annihilating its wildlife, and detested by native Highlanders, who have no opportunity of possessing the land they have lived on for centuries, and whose memory of the evictions is as solid as the link in a chain.

The misery of the Clearances involved not only the suffering of hardship, bullying and death, but the most terrible of all tragedies, the destruction of a people. It was the completion of the process begun at Culloden to undermine the Highlander's way of life and the ways he had of interpreting it: his customs and culture. That is why the Highland Clearances is Scotland's most forceful, clear and valuable myth. Throughout the entire country there is the sense that what took place in the Highlands during the earlier part of last century is a clue to what has happened to modern Scotland.

There have always been two ways of looking at the events of the Clearances and their effects, both on the immediate communities and on the nation. For simplicity, I will call them the view of the historian and the view of the poet.

Here is what the historian sees:

It is necessary to see all the events in the Sutherland clearances in a deeper perspective. Sutherland had never been as Donald Macleod painted it, a peasant Arcadia of rosy prosperity, plump girls and happy bakers. On the contrary it had for long been a county of poverty and emigration . . . The plan formulated by the chief land-agents to the Countess of Sutherland after 1807 was a serious and largely conventional attempt to recast the economy of an immense estate to the benefit of all parties involved. It was clear that the land had been badly managed in the past. To increase income from the estate the inland straths were to be rented to sheep farmers: to give the peasants a fair chance to revive their fortunes, they were to be resettled near the coast to fish and weave.

Here is what the poet sees:

I remember my grandmother, a sadly-dressed woman with a world of sorrow in her faded blue eyes, as if the shadow of the past were always upon her spirit. I never saw her smile, and when I asked my mother for the cause she told me that that look of pain came upon my grandmother's face with the fires of Strathnaver. Even when my grandmother was in her last illness, in May 1882, when the present was fading from her memory, she appeared again as a girl of twelve in Strathnaver, continually asking, 'Whose house is burning now?' and crying out now and again, 'Save the people!'

★   ★   ★

The Inverness to Thurso train picked me up at Helmsdale at nine minutes past nine in the morning.

Twenty miles on through the Strath of Kildonan, the train made a sharp turn to the right, then continued to Thurso. I was going to Bettyhill, which was north-west of there, and so had to disembark at Kinbrace and hope for a lift to take me thirty miles on. The train would stop at Kinbrace only by special arrangement with the guard, and so I sought him out once we started and he assured me that the engine would pause long enough for me to step down.

It was a weirdly beautiful journey through the heights of Kildonan, and once again I gladly would have extended it long beyond the time it lasted. Vestiges of steadings and lazybeds lay as bumps in the land along the length of the glen, here and there betrayed only by changes of shading in the earth. Very occasionally, a slightly grander house showed signs of continued habitation.

Sitting opposite was an old man with white hair and a weather-coloured face, his two walking sticks hooked on to the edge of the

5 Girls in the Waterloo Bar, in Aberdeen docks

6 George Kinloch of Kinloch, 'The Radical Laird' (From the collection of Sir John Kinloch Bart, of that Ilk)

7 Donald Macleod of Rossal. This portrait, a possible likeness, is in the collection of a relative of Macleod's

8 John McEwen, who wrote *Who Owns Scotland*, his first book, at the age of ninety

9 A descendant of the Badbea families

10 Kinbrace station

11 Badbea

12 Rockfield village

13 Portmahomack

table which separated us. I made some remark on the landscape and
he nodded his head in agreement, attaching his eyes to me. He was
a Strath Naver man, who had lived there all his life, and his
business was crofting. The night before he had been to Inverness
and this morning he was travelling to Thurso to consult with a
relative on some business matter. He lifted one of his walking sticks
and, smiling for the first time, shook it at me.

'It's not as easy as it used to be.'

He asked why I was travelling this way and I mentioned an
interest in the Clearances.

'Have you seen the museum at Bettyhill?'

'No, but I know about it and will see it when I'm there.'

'They should close it down, that's what they should do with it!'

'Why do you say that?'

'Because evictions is a thing of the past and they should leave
them there. It's all finished with now and there's no use in talking
about it all the time – evictions, evictions, evictions!'

I replied, somewhat feebly, that I could see no point in forgetting
about it either.

'That's what they *should* do, forget about it. We have good
proprietors up here now, that's the thing that matters, not the past,
the past!'

For the remainder of the journey we talked about other things
and then, as the train approached Kinbrace, I said goodbye and
went to stand by the door. The train slowed and finally paused. I
pulled down the window but the platform was not in sight and it
was a long way to the ground, so I waited.

Then I heard a cry which was plainly meant for me:

'KIN – BRA – ACE!'

Since it was clear that the train was going to move no further
along the track, there was only one thing to do if I was not to end
up in Thurso. I opened the door, dropped my bag about ten feet to
the ground, and then, to the amusement of the passengers left
behind in the carriage, jumped after it, stumbling and almost falling
over as I hit the ground. When I stood up nothing was sprained. A
second later, the train pulled off, revealing the platform on the
other side.

A postman was lifting up the mailbag from the platform where it had been dropped. From underneath his cocked hat, he regarded me sternly, standing in the sidings among weeds and nettles, picking up my own bag.

'You could've broke yer bloody neck, boy!' he called across the rails, shaking his head. 'If it was me was the guard I'd come over there and break it for you!'

I thanked him for his concern, and, feeling slightly daunted by my welcomes, walked out of the station on to the road.

I had been warned by the manager of the Bridge Hotel that it was a quiet road. It was so quiet that after half an hour I hadn't seen a car. The first one to pass had fishing rods on the roof-rack and German registration plates. The driver and his companion regarded me coolly and disappeared.

I thought of walking, but it would have been hopeless. The temperature was high in the seventies, and with my bag, not a backpack but one with handles, I could have advanced no more than a mile or two.

To my left, across a burn, the field ran upwards in a slight rise which the map told me was Tor na Craoibhe. On my other side, Tor du. Enveloped by earth and sky, a landscape of ineffable beauty and authority, I felt more lonely than at any time since I started out. I was conscious of only one sound: the irregular croaking of a frog, coming from the direction of a lazy burn guarding Tor na Craoibhe. At first I could not make out what it was, until I heard it again, and then again. Finally, I began to look for it, for company, but if I got close it stopped croaking. So I went back to the roadside, and after a few seconds heard it again, and had to be content with that.

It was at least another half-hour before a second vehicle appeared on the road. It was a red Land Rover – the post van. Somewhat hopelessly, I stuck out my thumb and met the eyes of the postman, and to my surprise he pulled to a halt and climbed out of his cabin.

'Didna know you was comin' wi' me, boy,' he said, and opened the back door of his van to let me in.

The parish of Farr, which includes Bettyhill, is Mackay country.

John K. Mackay was born there, it is very much his country, and he knows every inhabitant of Strath Naver.

He is small in height, about sixty years old, and gives an impression of never in his life having been fooled or got the bad side of a bargain. When we talked face to face, his eyes never left mine, while his brow registered changes in tone or emotion. He has always been a crofter, supplementing his income – as is the custom among crofters – formerly with his trade, which is stonemasonry, and now with the postman's round, which he does three days a week.

There is another postman and his name is also John Mackay. The John Mackays' duties entail the delivery of mail, newspapers and groceries, on the stretch of land between Kinbrace and Bettyhill, and many small roads besides, which means a call at virtually every house in Strath Naver, about twenty of them.

At first, when I asked questions from my place among the groceries in the back of the van, John K. Mackay was reticent. He told me later he had suspected me of being a Post Office spy.

'This is all Highland Clearances country, isn't it?'

'It is.'

There followed a pause. For something else to say, I mentioned my journey through the heights of Kildonan.

'You're interested in this business, are you? Well, you'll see a lot more evidence of it when we go up through Strath Naver.'

John Mackay began to talk. He talked so much that he overlooked some of his messages on the way to Bettyhill, and left a pint of milk and two copies of *Woman's Own* undelivered.

'It's still very much alive in the hearts of the people up here, the Clearances. You'll have heard of the museum up in Bettyhill?'

'That's one of the reasons I'm going there.'

'Oh, is it now? Well, I'm one o' the trustees o' it.'

As we drove on he pointed out places whose names were familiar to me only from books, and reminded me of the events associated with them; in the many eye-witness accounts of the Sutherland Clearances (the most notorious, in a method of depopulation which swept the Highlands), the same pitiful tales recur: of blazing homesteads and townships, of aged widows dragged from burning houses and dying within days, of old men taking to the woods and wandering about in a state of insanity, of a return to the native parish to find deserted wastelands: '*O, chan eil ach sgiala bronach! sgiala bronach!*' 'Oh, only sad news, sad news!' 'The whole of the inhabitants of Kildonan, numbering nearly two thousand souls, except three families, were utterly rooted and burnt out, and the whole parish converted into a solitary wilderness.' 'Their plan of operations was to clear the cottages of their inmates, giving them about half an hour to pack up and carry off their furniture, and then set the cottages on fire.'

One man saved a few pieces of timber from his house and took them down to the River Naver where he made a raft out of them, intending to float downstream to safety and there build a hut for himself and his family. But the gang spotted him and followed him and set fire to the beams.

The leading villain in the saga of the Sutherland Clearances is Patrick Sellar, the factor for the House of Sutherland. In 1816 he was charged at Inverness with culpable homicide and fire-raising in connection with the evictions, but was 'honourably acquitted'. At Syre, we came to his house, a small white building with a red roof.

'Go and burn it down!' said John Mackay.

The source book on the Sutherland Clearances is *Gloomy Memories*, by Donald Macleod, an eye-witness account written many years after the events it describes, filled with rage and indignation. It is, ostensibly, a reply to the *Sunny Memories* of Harriet Beecher Stowe, which was a vindication of the Sutherland 'improvements'. The author's name was familiar to me, not only from his own book, but also because he received a poignant mention in another book, *The Trial of Patrick Sellar*, by Ian Grimble:

On the summit of Ben Bhraggie, already such a conspicuous landmark above the castle of Dunrobin, a huge statue of the Duke of Sutherland was erected by order of his widow and her factor. The thoughtful and retiring Duke gazes in effigy over the county he occasionally visited, and whose name he adopted for six short months. But Donald Macleod has no memorial.

From Syre, John turned the van southwards. He had some deliveries to make at Dal Harrald. The road paralleled the River

Naver, which has its source in Loch Naver, just beyond the tiny settlement. John said he would let me off, make his delivery at Dal Harrald and then pick me up on the way back. He thought I ought to have a good look at the river; it was the finest river he knew; and there was something else he wished to show me.

At the spot where we stopped, beside a small monument, the river ran about thirty feet wide. It was shallow due to the lack of rain and we could see some small fish keeping close to the bank. On the other side was a spruce forest which, however, did not cover the hill, stopping about halfway up in a neat fringe, leaving the crest bald. On that part I could see the ruins of the village of Rossal, which were far more extensive than any others I had seen either in Strath Naver or the Strath of Kildonan.

John said he would take me there within the next day or two, if I cared to hang around. Then he led me along the bank towards the short stocky monument. It was made from bricks and mortar, and had a bronze plaque:

IN MEMORY OF
DONALD MACLEOD

STONEMASON

Who witnessed the
destruction of Rossal
in 1814 and wrote 'Gloomy Memories'

He read the words aloud and then told me to wait while he went to Dal Harrald.

'Are there many live along there?'

'Only one: a shepherd, name of Anderson. A Lowland name, you see, but a nice man nevertheless.'

While he was gone I inspected the monument closely and then sat by the river. Birds flew low over the surface and dragonflies hovered above the shallows. Twenty minutes later, a red speck appeared, humming through the heat haze. John climbed out of the Land Rover and came and stood by the monument and ran the fingers of one hand over the bronze plaque.

'Well then, what do you think of it?'

I asked who had built it and he regarded me with surprise.

'I did.'

★   ★   ★

'This is a dying community you're seeing here. I make no apology for saying that to you. My father worked the croft, *his* father worked it, but my son won't do it. All the people you meet on the way up through the strath – what do you notice that they all have in common? They're all old people, that's right. Hardly a child under fifty among them; a community of retired crofters. And if their places are filled, it's by incomers – white settlers, we call them.

'You remember that woman with the two children we spoke to? Well, her house is just up back of where we stopped to speak to her, but she's not living in it just now. She hasn't been living in it for the last month. She lives in a caravan while her own house is let to holidaymakers. That's the way they make a wee bit extra for themselves up here, you see. Everybody round here needs something to make that wee bit extra. I do the post round, she gives her house away.'

John Mackay was a reckless driver. He commandeered the whole of the narrow road which traversed Strath Naver, expecting to meet few cars. On the occasions when one did pass us coming from the other direction, he manoeuvred the Land Rover to the left-hand side of the road with such wrenching and cursing that the first time I thought we had stuck in a ditch. This ruthless method of getting the mail through was made even more hazardous by the constant rush of opinions which flew from his tongue.

Could he speak the Gaelic, I asked. Yes he could, certainly he could, he spoke it whenever the opportunity arose; he could neither read it nor write it, only speak it. It gave him, he said, a connection.

A connection with what?

'Well, you see now, the name of this place.' We were approaching the village at last. 'Bettyhill. They'll tell you it's named for the Countess of Sutherland, Elizabeth. But you see that's not the name in Gaelic, Bettyhill. The Gaelic name is Am Blaran Odhar, the grey bog. Nothing to do with your Countess of Sutherland, nothing at

all. Do you think I want to live in a place named after the Countess?
Do I hell! No, I want to live in the place where my people came to,
the place where she sent them – the grey bog.

'Come with me later and I'll show you the piles of stones the
people had to clear off their plots up there on the coast before they
could even get a weed to grow on them. And this "Bettyhill" – I'll
tell you where it comes from: there used to be a woman lived here by
herself on a hill, and that hill became known as Betty Cnoc, which
means Betty's Hill, and they named it after her. *That's* how the grey
bog got called Bettyhill.'

We passed the sign with the names in English and Gaelic printed
on it. On the ragged crown of Great Britain, Bettyhill is the focal
point of Strath Naver. Besides being pretty, it is strangely patterned,
with houses widely scattered across low hills. At first glance, it
appears to have no centre. A general store sells newspapers,
groceries and liquor, and also doubles as a post office; across the
road, one hundred yards away, is the hotel with its public bar. This is
the village centre.

John pointed out his croft to me: it was high up on a hill, at least
half a mile away. Beyond the post office, the street declines to a quick
valley, where sits Farr Parish Church – now the Strath Naver
Museum – before rising to a crop of roads which lead to outlying
groups of crofts, such as Swordly, Kirktomy and Clerkhill.

After completing his business at the post office, John offered to
buy me a drink. We walked across the road to the public bar of the
hotel, an austere, barn-like structure, without ornament or design.
Inside, he ordered two pints of beer.

'And you'll have a dram?'

'No, thanks.' It was just past noon.

'And two drams.'

We were joined by another local man. John offered to buy him a
drink, but he insisted on buying one for us instead. I had not yet
finished my first, so on accepting his offer, requested a half pint only.

'Three pints and three drams.'

Naturally, John knew everyone who entered the pub, a dangerous
privilege, since in these parts to say 'no' to a drink is to give not an
answer but an offence. It required some tactical play to avoid a quick

passage to oblivion. The only way to get out of accepting yet
another drink was to insist on paying for the new round yourself,
and then ensure that your own glass was not filled.

John Mackay was spoken of with respect by everyone at the
bar.

'He's the man who dips everyone else's sheep.'

'He never sits down, not for a minute.'

'He should take it more easy, he's retirement age, you know.
But it's dawn to dusk with him, nothing less.'

'Four pints and four drams.'

I ordered a plate of fish and chips to fortify my stomach.

'Make his a double.'

'Oh, I'll have none of it.'

'None of it is what you won't have. Make it four doubles.'

'And four pints. I'm paying.'

'Nev-er!'

'I better take this man away from here. He'll be saying I've got
him into bad company.'

'And so you have.'

'Well, here's his health.'

'Aye, and your own.'

'And again?'

It was not yet one o'clock. John, having initially bought a
round only for us two, naturally had to buy another, and then I
too was eager to protect my reputation.

'No, no, not for me,' John said when asked what he would
have.

The other man shook his head and a third looked away shyly as
I offered.

'Four pints and four drams.'

Eventually, we reached a natural break in the proceedings,
which until then had looked as if they might continue for ever,
and we were able to make an exit without loss of honour.

'You're comin' home wi' me, boy. Get some dinner inside you
and you can meet my wife.'

'But I've just eaten.'

'Well, you can eat some more!'

We drove down and up the valley to John Mackay's croft. It sat on the coast on a rise overlooking Farr Point and the North Sea, with none of the neighbours closer than fifty yards. Chickens scattered as he parked the Land Rover. From the driver's cabin, he brought a pair of large wellington boots, and we went inside the low cottage.

Margaret Mackay was an ample, curly-headed woman with an angelic voice, which she used sparingly. A fry-up was waiting on the stove for John, and on seeing the unannounced guest, Margaret immediately moved to supplement it with another chop and two eggs. But John stopped her. He lifted one of the wellingtons from the floor, held it in the air, and with his other hand ceremoniously withdrew a pink and silver salmon.

Margaret released a long 'ooooh' sound.

John Mackay held up the salmon triumphantly.

Margaret applied her kitchen knife, trimming first the head, and then three large-hearted steaks.

★ ★ ★

Afterwards, I went to look round the Strath Naver Museum. It was a small place, opened quite recently, with a modest but expanding collection of exhibits.

Three items struck me as being of particular interest. One was a reference to a report in the Proceedings of the Society of Antiquaries for Scotland on the excavation of Rossal, which stated that the excavators had found no evidence to support the allegations of burnings by the factors, which are contained in every eye-witness account.

The second was these lines from a manuscript poem addressed to Donald Macleod, by a local poet:

> So sleep on Macleod, the long sleep of the just,
> The tyrant's bones lie also in the dust,
> Their names and poisonous sting, where'er they're heard.
> In Highland hearts, Macleod, your name is revered.

Finally, a clipping from a Caithness newspaper in which the letter-writer complained of the lack of mention of cleared settlements on Ordnance Survey maps. He listed the names of some of the places he

had in mind: Rossal, Syre, Mowdale, Baghardy, Blairdow, Rhec-
opag, Nibad, Acheness, Chiltrick, Rhimisdale, Auldinarve, Achadh
An Eas, Ach a Chuil, Ceann Na Coille, Kedsary, Langdale.

★   ★   ★

Rossal was probably the largest of these, housing roughly thirteen
families. It is fourteen miles down the strath from Bettyhill, on the
east bank of the wide, brown River Naver. John Mackay dropped
me at Rhimisdale at eight o'clock next morning, before continuing
on his way to collect the mail at Kinbrace, and I walked about a mile
along a track until reaching an opening in the wood which led
through the trees to Rossal. It was built on Beinn Rosail, one of the
highest points on the ridge called the heights of Naver, and runs in a
slope towards the river. Although the presence of a souterrain within
its confines suggests settlement since pre-historic times, the earliest
documentary reference to Rossal occurs in 1296, when fifty acres of
arable land was granted to Sir Reginald de Chen by the Bishop of
Moray.

Donald Macleod, born the son of a farmer in or about 1799, was
one of the last generation of inhabitants. Having the trade of
stonemason, he frequently travelled to Edinburgh in the summer
months to earn money, where he learned to read and write English
better than any other member of his social class in a county
populated mainly by what one of the factors of the House of
Sutherland called 'mountain savages'.

In 1814, Rossal was cleared, like all the other villages in the strath,
to make way for a sheep run. Donald Macleod resisted these actions
more steadfastly than did the others, and as a result of his
independent mind he became a marked man in the eyes of the
Sutherland agents, to the extent of being hounded for debts which,
by his own account, had been paid in full.

In October 1830, one month after his skirmish with the authorities
over his supposed debts, his wife was evicted from their home. After
the death of his father-in-law, Donald had assumed responsibility
for six orphans, which made his excursions to find work more
necessary and more frequent. It was during one of those absences
that a party of eight men arrived at the house and evicted his wife and

children, throwing out the furniture and nailing up doors and windows after them. She was told by the factor that he could do things 'which would astonish her' and the inhabitants of the strath were warned against 'affording shelter or assistance to wife, child or animal belonging to Donald Macleod'. The woman and her children were left to sleep outside in the autumn weather until, at length, she was given shelter by a man in Armidale, he himself leaving the house to avoid recrimination when the inevitable eviction followed – as it did, once more when her husband was absent. This time Mrs Macleod tried to walk to Thurso to join him, but the journey unsettled her mind, leaving her, in his words, 'a living monument of Highland oppression'.

The following year Donald Macleod emigrated to Canada, where he became a bookseller in Ontario. In 1840, the *Edinburgh Evening Chronicle* began to publish a series of his letters, telling of his experiences during the Strath Naver Clearances, and in 1857, when the author was approaching the age of sixty, these were expanded to form *Gloomy Memories*. The addressee is Harriet Beecher Stowe.

In 1841, when I published my first pamphlet, I paid $4.50c, for binding of one of them, in a splendid style, which I sent by mail to his Grace the present Duke of Sutherland, with a complimentary note requesting him to peruse it, and let me know if it contained anything offensive or untrue. I never received a reply, nor did I expect it; yet I am satisfied that his Grace did peruse it. I posted a copy of it to Mr Loch, his chief commissioner; to Mr W. Mackenzie, his chief lawyer in Edinburgh; to every one of their underlings, to sheep farmers, and ministers in the county of Sutherland, who abetted the depopulators, and I challenged the whole of them, and other literary scourges who aided and justified their unhallowed doings, to gainsay one statement I have made. Can you or any other believe that a poor sinner like Donald Macleod would be allowed for so many years to escape with impunity, had he been circulating and publishing calumnious, absurd falsehoods against such personages as the House of Sutherland? No, I tell you, if money could secure my punishment, without establishing their own shame and guilt, that it would be considered well-spent long ere now, – they would eat me in penny pies if they could get me cooked for them.

I agree with you that the Duchess of Sutherland is a beautiful, accomplished lady, who would shudder at the idea of taking a faggot or a burning torch in her hand to set fire to the cottages of her tenants, and so would her predecessor, the first Duchess of Sutherland, her good mother; likewise would the late and present Dukes of Sutherland, at least I am willing to believe that they would. Yet it was done in their name, under their authority, to their knowledge, and with their sanction. The dukes and duchesses of Sutherland, and those of their depopulating order, had not, nor have they any call to defile their pure work in milder work than to burn people's houses; no, no, they had, and have plenty of willing tools at their beck to perform their dirty work. Whatever amount of humanity and purity of heart the late or present Duke or Duchess may possess or be ascribed to them, we know the class of men from whom they selected their commissioners, factors, and underlings. I knew every one of the unrighteous servants who ruled the Sutherland estate for the last fifty years, and I am justified in saying that the most skilful phrenologist and physiognomist that ever existed could not discern one spark of humanity in the whole of them, from Mr Loch down to Donald Sgrios, or Damnable Donald, the name by which the latter was known. The most of those cruel executors of the atrocities I have been describing are now dead, and to be feared but not lamented. But it seems their chief was left to give you all the information you required about British slavery and oppression. I have read from speeches delivered by Mr Loch at public dinners among his own party, 'that he would never be satisfied until the Gaelic language and the Ga·lic people would be extirpated root and branch from the Sutherland estate; yes, from the Highlands of Scotland' . . .

I was at the pulling down and burning of the house of William Chisolm. I got my hands burnt taking out the poor old woman from amidst the flames of her once-comfortable though humble dwelling, and a more horrifying and lamentable scene could scarcely be witnessed. I may say the skeleton of a once tall, robust high-cheek-boned, respectable woman, who had seen better days; who could neither hear, see, nor speak; without a tooth in her mouth, her cheek skin meeting in the centre, her eyes sunk out of sight in their sockets, her mouth wide open, her nose standing upright among smoke and flames, uttering piercing moans of distress and agony, in articulations from which could be only understood, 'Oh, Dhia, Dhia, teine, teine – Oh, God, God, fire, fire.' When she came to the pure air, her bosom heaved to a most extraordinary degree, accompanied by a deep, hollow sound from her lungs, comparable to the sound of thunder at a distance. When laid down upon the bare, soft, moss floor of the roofless shed, I will never forget the foam of perspiration which emitted and covered the pallid death-looking countenance. This was a scene, madam, worthy of an artist's pencil, and of a conspicuous place on the stages of tragedy. Yet you call this a specimen of the ridiculous stories which found their way into the respectable prints, because Mr Loch, the chief actor, told you that Sellar, the head executive, brought an action against the sheriff and obtained a verdict for heavy damages. What a subterfuge; but it will not answer the purpose. '*The bed is too short to stretch yourself, and the covering too narrow and short to cover you.*' If you took the information and evidence upon which you founded your *Uncle Tom's Cabin* from such unreliable sources, who can believe the one-tenth of your novel? I cannot.

. . . Had you the opportunity, madam, of seeing the scenes which I and hundreds more have seen – the wild ferocious appearance of the infamous *gang* who constituted the burning party, covered their face and hands with soot and ashes of the burning houses, cemented by torch-grease and their own sweat, kept continually drunk or half-drunk while at work; and to observe the hellish amusements some of them would get up for themselves and for an additional pleasure to their leaders! The people's houses were generally built upon declivities, and in many cases not far from pretty steep precipices. They preserved their meal in tight-made boxes, or chests, as they were called, and when this fiendish party found any quantity of meal, they would carry it between them to the brink, and dispatch it down the precipice amidst shrieks and yells. It was considered grand sport to see the box breaking to atoms and the meal mixed with the air. When they would set fire to a house, they would watch any of the domestic animals making their escape from the flames, such as dogs, cats, hens, or any poultry; these were caught and thrown back to the flames – grand sport for demons in human form!

During his 'exposure' he received many letters of encouragement 'from almost every quarter of the empire and her colonies'. He died, an unsuccessful bookseller, in Woodstock, Ontario, in 1860.

Next to nothing is known about any other inhabitant of Rossal, about how the children looked, whether healthy or half-starved, if the men were indolent, as some historical rumours have it. Macleod's eulogies on the living Rossal, as opposed to his elegies on the dead one, are sketchy and have often been rejected as romantic pictures: 'Sutherland had never been . . . a peasant Arcadia', as the historian put it. Yet, in accounts of the people's mode of living before the Clearances took place, it is invariably the parties who have an interest in their removal who lament their 'misery' the

loudest; the few voices which history has given the people themselves – Donald Macleod's first among them – speak differently. It is
also curious that the men of the Highland villages such as Rossal have
two conflicting reputations which seem to be current at the same
time: supposedly idlers at home, when fighting abroad in the French
wars they gained a reputation for courage and skill which spread
across the world.

'They were men!' Eckermann told Goethe, having seen the
Highlanders of the 93rd regiment before the Battle of Waterloo.
'All strong, nimble and free as if they had come straight from the
hand of God. They carried their heads so freely and gaily and
marched so lightly, swinging along with their bare knees, that
you would have thought they had never heard of original sin or
the primal curse.'

The same men returned home afterwards to their native straths to
find their villages burned to the ground.

From the crest of Beinn Rosail, the lay-out of the village below
took on a pattern. There were eighteen longhouses, accommodating
roughly one hundred people. They kept poultry and black (Highland) cattle, for milk and cheese. In times of severe hardship the cattle
were bled and their blood was mixed with oats to make a kind of
porridge which was fried and eaten. Their most valuable non-edible
resource was peat, which has four levels, each level having a different
use: top for insulation, middle for houses and dykes, lower for fuel,
and at the deepest level, hardened pine with which to make beams
for houses. These beams, which were extremely valuable in an
almost treeless country, were handed down through the generations, and it was these which the tenants sought to protect first
when the 'fire and crow-bar brigade' arrived. There are accounts of
Sellar and his men prohibiting their removal and insisting that they
be burned instead.

From the summit of the slight incline, across the patterns of
stones, across the rutted surfaces of the peat bogs still visible, the
only sound was the River Naver. The monument which the
stonemason-postman raised to the stonemason-author was a dot on
the opposite bank, and the bright red corrugated-iron roof of Sellar's
house at Syre was in view.

III

We were always in the habit of conversing with the Highlanders, with whom one comes so much in contact in the Highlands.

Queen Victoria

It is quite easy to spend a week on an estate some-where in the Highlands and never see a single Scot, far less talk to one – except of course the gillie, a pet name for a gamekeeper which derives from the Gaelic *gille*, meaning 'boy'. Anyone seeking an answer to why the Scots continue to resent the English in the traditional manner need look no further than this bizarre equation.

John Mackay called the shooting lodges 'the curse o' the High-lands', as he drove me down Strath Naver once again, to leave me at Kinbrace. Frequently, when he caught sight of someone walking by the side of the road, or standing outside a house, he would stop for a chat; I knew that on the way back up he would stop at every house, as before, whether he had a delivery to make or not.

He put me down at the station and we shook hands.

'I liked you when I first saw you,' he said. 'I knew you were all right when I saw you get down off that train on the wrong side.'

We parted and I crossed the railway track. Since no train would be travelling in my direction for another four hours, I chose a likely spot where it would be easy for drivers to pull in, and waited for a car.

It was a long time before the first one came into view. It glided down the hill from the north, slowed to a walking pace and the driver sized me up before reaching a dead halt.

'Where are you going?'

'Helmsdale.'

'Okay, hop in.'

It was a good lift. The Englishman behind the wheel owned not only the car he was driving but the road he was travelling and the land it crossed, beyond every horizon; a large slice, in fact, of the county of Sutherland.

I took an instant liking to the Laird of A —— , not least because of his kindness in plucking me out of my hopeless predicament on the road. He said at first that he would drop me a few miles this side of

Helmsdale, but in the end he went out of his way to drive me not only there but fifteen miles further on.

The road snaked through the Strath of Kildonan, keeping parallel with both river and railway track. On each side we passed a panorama of low green hills and yellowy grouse moors, occasionally interrupted by a chunk of spruce forest. On the banks of the river grew whins and young trees; here and there a line of peats, piled into chimneys, stood out on a hill. Protruding from the open roof was a fishing rod – the Laird was going fishing in his river.

'What do you hope to catch?'

'Salmon. Not much chance of that, sadly.'

'No?'

'Well, you can see how low the river is, for one thing. We need some rain very badly. This sunshine's all right for you, but it doesn't help the poor fish. But the main problem is poachers. They make real trouble around here. Do you know, there has been a seventy per cent depletion in salmon stocks this year. Seventy per cent. That's a catastrophic figure by any measure.'

'Do you ever catch any of the poachers?'

'Sometimes, but you'll never catch them all. They've got their nets all over the place, up and down the river.'

'Do you live up here all the year round?'

'I wish I did, I dearly wish I did. I will soon, of course, after I've retired. Then my son can start to do all the hard work.'

The total land area of the county of Sutherland is 1,297,803 acres, out of which the present Countess owns 123,500 (as Mrs Janson she owns a further 34,500 acres). Compared with the 1,201,000 acres which the Sutherland family owned in 1874, this is a big drop but, as John McEwen, the author of *Who Owns Scotland* says, 'still comfortable'.

In the 1870s, the Sutherland estate excluded the presence of any other major landowner in the county, whereas today there are fifteen estates above 24,000 acres, and my driver owned one of them. He did not tell me how many people were housed on this area, but it would be unlikely to be more than the number of cattle, which is sixty. There are also 2,000 sheep – one for every twelve acres. The main activity for which the land is utilised, on this estate as on most others, is shooting and stalking.

The Laird of A —— told me about a gillie he had had to get rid of recently, speaking of it as a distasteful episode on an otherwise untroubled estate. Not for him summary evictions: 'We gave him several chances.' The shepherds, on the other hand, had been with the family for several generations.

'The Highland Clearances was one of those plans where the basic conception was sound, but the execution of it – because the Countess's main man was a crook – was a shambles. You see, the Countess only visited her estates once or twice a year. After that, she left it all in the hands of Sellar, and Sellar was a brute.

'But the economics of the plan were quite fair: move the people on to the coast and build factories for them there – because inland they were living in the most sordid conditions. But in the end, you see, the fish factories never materialised, and the conditions of these people worsened. While they had previously been able to farm their small plots of land – even if what they got from them was inadequate – now they had virtually nothing at all. And of course, some of them died and some of them emigrated, and . . . It really was a dreadful shame. Improvements were desperately needed, though. You must try to understand, these people were living in the most *dire* poverty.'

He stopped the car suddenly but gently. A thin line of deer was disappearing behind the crest of a hill. The Laird's practised eye had picked them out, though they were only a shadow and he was driving with care, while mine had missed them.

'Isn't that a beautiful sight,' he said in a low voice, as though afraid of disturbing the animals half a mile away. They had paused in unison at the top of the hill and gazed along the strath.

'*The* most beautiful sight, I sometimes think, a line of deer on a high hill . . . '

His foot released the clutch pedal and we started our lazy progress once more.

'Ever go stalking? I still do. I love stalking but I can never fire the final shot any more. Isn't that funny? I can't be the executioner.'

7
Invisible Ink

In the dress of the fool, the two colours that have tormented me – English and Gaelic, black and red, the court of injustice, the reason for my anger, and that fine rain from the mountains and those grievous storms from my mind streaming the two colours together so that I will go with my poor sight in the one colour that is so odd that the King himself will not understand my conversation.

Iain Crichton Smith,
'The Fool'
(translated from the Gaelic by the author)

I

Three lifts carried me across country to Oban next day.

The east and west coasts of Scotland are separate countries, yet no more than two or three hours is required to reach one from the other at virtually any point along the length of the land. The physiognomy of each displays its character: east, mild and frank, unimaginative at times, occasionally verging on dullness; west, brooding, creative, liable to extremes, naturally domineering.

There are also distinct differences between counties. My first lift came from a Caithness driver who was travelling from Helmsdale to Inverness in a Sherpa van. I mentioned my time in Bettyhill and he approved, nodding his head, and spoke of his neighbours as if they lived on the opposite shore of a wide ocean.

'They're good people, the Sutherland people,' he advised me earnestly.

Next, I went sixty-two miles with an RAF engineer on leave. An intense, moustachioed young man who had signed on for twenty-two years' service, he wore reflecting sunglasses, although the sky had at last clouded over, and spoke through closed lips. Harsh Rolling Stones music crowded the compact saloon, causing each of us to say 'What?' when the other asked a question. He was bound for Fort William and was going to spend his holiday rock-climbing.

'Alone?' I bawled.

His fingers reached for volume control.

'Alone?'

He nodded. When I asked him to explain what drew him to his sport, he shrugged, said something about 'a feeling', and turned the music up again.

'It's the only way to live,' I heard him say.

We travelled in silence until I happened on his other favourite subject: nuclear war.

He told me of 'constant preparations' within the forces, that his officers banked on a war lasting three days, with a six-month recovery period, which gave us, according to some reasoning I was unable to follow, 'a fifty-fifty chance'. He added that although it was his ambition to participate in a major war, he did not share this particular view.

'Do you argue with them?'

'Of course not. I do what I'm told.'

'Are you scared?'

'No,' in a clipped voice.

'Would you like to have been in the Falklands?'

'I'd have given my right arm.'

Outside Fort William, I left him to his mountains and his feeling.

My third lift came almost immediately. It was given by a young woman who drove heart-stoppingly to Oban. She was intense and even more stubbornly against conversation than the last. Dark clouds that had pondered all morning and threatened me with spits as I stood by the side of the road, now began to rain heavily. The car's wipers were faulty, only half-clearing the hard drops that lashed against the windscreen, which made me more nervous than did the combination of silence and speed. She did not live in Oban and was not going to stay there, but was headed for a reunion with her boyfriend, a lighthouse keeper, who was working fifteen miles out.

'I suppose it gets lonely.'

She replied that it suited him.

'He doesn't like company much.'

I tried to imagine the two of them, out at sea, with savage waves surrounding them, solitary in their silent tower, enjoying life.

★   ★   ★

I had two immediate missions in the west: one was to call on the poet and novelist Iain Crichton Smith, who lives in Oban; the other was to land on the island of Iona, at the tip of the long, fat finger of Mull – the Ross – which forms a bridge between Iona and the port of Oban.

Oban is a busy town, with many boats in its bracket-shaped harbour; the hills of several different islands are visible from the bay. I walked around in the rain and knocked on several doors before finding somebody prepared to take me in, and then only just.

The landlady dried her hands on her apron and used one finger to flick aside a lock of hair.

'No room, doc,' she said quickly – and then, easing slightly, 'It's the wrong time of year.' At the back of her voice was an Irish girl. I was about to retreat once again, but slowly, for I sensed a softening of her resistance.

'Is it just the one night, doc?'

I said it was: I would be sailing to Mull in the morning. She smoothed her apron with outstretched fingers and looked me over once more.

'Ah well, come on in then. That's a cold wind blowing out there and it's no weather to be walking out in.' She stood back and waited until I was over the threshold before adding: 'You won't mind if I have to put another fellow in beside you, will you? It's a double room, you see, doc.' Concern must have jigged my features, for she reassured me quickly: 'I'll make sure it's not one of them dirty types, doc, with the long hair or such things.'

She was already halfway up the stairs and I followed automatically. The decor was pre-war, with yellowing flowery wallpaper, linoleum on the floors, and every wooden fitment stained dark brown. The room itself was spacious, with one wooden bed which, though unusually wide, did nothing to reconcile me to the thought of having to share it with 'another fellow'.

Mrs Kelly charged four pounds a night, which was about the cheapest accommodation I had found, but the windows rattled in the frames and the cold wind came through the pane. The room gave directly on to the harbour, with a view of the opposite heel of the bay; some pale-green hills, which I took to be Mull, loured in the mist. I left the house to go out into the wet streets.

Iain Crichton Smith (Iain Mac a'Ghobhainn) was for many years the head teacher of English at Oban High School, and has continued to live in the town since he retired early to spend all his time writing. He is a poet of double vision, 'black and red', English and Gaelic, 'the two colours that have tormented me', and this duality is reflected in the actual content of his work, which is often generated by an internal debate. Gaelic is his first language and the one he uses most naturally. In the Gaelic poems, such as 'The Fool', a whole culture appears to be crowding the poet's mind, which is filtered through image and symbol to emerge as the poem; whereas when he writes in English, the language, no matter how carefully managed, is often a mere vehicle for thought. The separation has caused him confusion and also grief.

I first became aware of Iain Crichton Smith as anything more than a name among many names of Scottish poets when, as a student, I attended a talk he gave in Edinburgh on the subject of religion. The particular brand of Protestantism he grew up with is that of the Free Church, which broke away from the established Church of Scotland in 1843, under the leadership of Thomas Chalmers; its rigid Calvinism was even more unyielding than that of the other, and it continues to be the dominant church in many Highland parishes today.

It was immediately evident that day in Edinburgh that the subject was not one about which he could speak dispassionately. The Free Church, he said, had played a major, mainly destructive part in his life, especially his early life on the island of Lewis, where he was born. As he elaborated, he grew angry and agitated, as if he were now confronted with a group of Free Church members and for the first time had the opportunity of telling them what he thought.

It was when the questions from the audience began that he really impressed me, however, with his willingness to admit uncertainty. In fact, Smith had no definite answers for anyone, although it was very clear he had thought deeply about every question he was asked, and even in the process of trying to answer, here and now, was continuing what must be an everlasting inner debate. I recognised it as the mark of a thinking man to be able to say 'I don't know'.

It was through a later reading of his work – and also through listening to Gaelic songs, of which I understood no words – that I realised that Gaelic was a missing part of my world, since with the modern Gael I share a history but not a language. The first thought consequent upon this discovery was, naturally, to begin immediately to learn the language, but what I sought could not be recovered in that way. Yet his history remains mine: written into my conscience in invisible ink, in a language I have forgotten how to understand.

I rang Iain Crichton Smith from a call-box on the promenade and he invited me round straight away. He is slight, with a bald head and bright eyes, and his face is ready and youthful, belying his fifty-five years. He has a steep forehead which is occasionally worried by a concertina brow. He pronounces his words 'as read': 'occasionally', for example, would have six clear syllables. His character is partly expressed in the evidence of careless shaving and crumpled clothes. He admits quite freely to being the world's worst typist, and editors frequently return his manuscripts with a note to say that they will be only too glad to read his latest work when a legible copy is produced. He laughs about this side of himself, and it is possible to see it as an effect of his most engaging attribute: an absence of self-importance.

When I called he was in the process of moving from the tenement flat where he lived – an experience which proved traumatic for him – and the afternoon gloom of the untidy living room was cheered by one bare light bulb. A wooden chair was found for me, then he disappeared into the kitchen, emerging with two glasses and a bottle. Over the following eight hours he talked about many things, the conversation frequently returning to his major preoccupations.

In Lewis, and in other areas dominated by the Free Church, it is sternly disapproved of to indulge as much energy, on a Sunday, as it takes to go for a walk, or swim, or shave, or even to rescue an endangered farm animal; also it is thought to be sinful to watch television or read a book (other than The Book). Efforts to establish a ferry service on a Sunday between the island and the mainland, have in the past led to demonstrations by ministers lying down before the gangplank.

'Here's a story for you,' said Iain. 'I was once in a house on Lewis, staying for a weekend. It was a wet Sunday afternoon and I was reading a novel. I stood up to go to the bathroom and left the novel on my chair, face down, and when I came back it was gone and in its place there was a pamphlet called "Bloody Thoughts". And in another house I went to once, I was carrying a large bottle of whisky with me which an American friend had given me as a present. When we arrived at this house – it wasn't even a Sunday – the woman who owned it said, "Thank you, I'll take that." And that was the last we ever saw of it.'

His fist closed and a look came into his face which I recognised from the day I had first seen him in Edinburgh.

'When I see one of these Free Church ministers on the street in Lewis, I feel like walking across the road and *hitting* him in the face!' His brow folded. 'I really do. It's power they want, that's all it is.'

When he spoke about the Gaelic language a note of melancholy entered his speech, which may be deepened by the knowledge of the part he has played in reinvigorating it. It is a feeling which is reflected in his poetry:

> Tinkers subdued to council houses learn
> to live as others do, earn as they earn,
> and English growing as the Gaelic dies
> describes these vast and towering island skies.
> God is surrendering to other gods
> as the stony moor to multiplying roads.

Finally, when it was time to leave, near midnight, he was still questioning. A reviewer had called into question his contribution to an anthology of critical essays on MacDiarmid, saying that Mr Crichton Smith did not give any indication of being acquainted with the latest developments in MacDiarmid criticism.

'I don't think it's necessary to be acquainted with the "latest developments" in anything to make an honest response, do you?'

As he wished me a safe passage through the rain to Mrs Kelly's, he said, to sum up our evening's talk, 'Do you not, like me, get more and more bewildered by the . . . ' He paused, until he hit upon the word in English: 'mult-i-far-i-ous-ness of things?'

My legs carried me back to Mrs Kelly's guest house, an unresisting passenger, along the rim of the harbour, past the station, through the dark. All the lights were out, though the front door had been left unlocked. I climbed the stairs with the help of my hands, as silently as I could, and at the top groped for the handle. With a sense of achievement, I fell on to the bed, not having had the alertness to check first and see if half of it was occupied by 'another fellow'.

★   ★   ★

Next morning, Mrs Kelly's house was a babel.

I met her on the stairs between my room and the bathroom, which was on the half-landing. When she saw me, she wished me a good morning, hoped I had a hearty appetite, and descended once more to the kitchen, talking all the time.

The bathroom door was unlocked. I pushed it open and to my surprise looked upon a large, hirsute man slowly drying himself after a bath. He said, quite calmly, 'Good morning', before I managed to apologise and retreat downstairs.

Breakfast was served in a large sitting room with a bay window facing the harbour. One half of it was reserved for the broad, circular table, on which were crowded packets of cereals, fruit juices, condiments, cutlery, and everything else required to feed several people, while the other half, including the area surrounding the fireplace, was packed with old furniture. A three-piece suite huddled close to the fire, and backing against the wall was a large sideboard which held plates, two tea sets neatly arranged as if tea were about to be served, framed photographs, copies of the *Reader's Digest*, an encroaching aspidistra, a table lamp on either side, and several ornaments of the 'Souvenir from Oban' type. The mantelpiece was similarly crowded, and so was a small wooden trolley which meekly cowered before the window. On the walls were several pictures: portraits, landscapes with Highland cattle, and an engraving of Oban harbour. Hardly an inch of space had not been utilised to hold something.

Mrs Kelly entered and asked me what I would like to start my breakfast. Before I had a chance to answer, she gave me a lecture on the calorie value of each of the cereals on parade before me.

'I'll have corn flakes.'

'Corn flakes has little in it good for you, doc.'

'Oh? Well, I'll try the All-Bran in that case.'

'All-Bran won't help you keep the plate of ham and eggs I've got coming for you.'

To this disquieting news, she appended the advice: 'Try a fruit juice, doc.'

The other guests trickled in and each was instructed as to the relative merits of the food they chose before being given fruit juice. One couple had a child who talked incessantly to Mrs Kelly and cried when his mother tried to force feed him with an egg. My head ached with last night's whisky. The man from the bathroom entered and Mrs Kelly treated him as if he were a son. He was a gruff, humourless man of about twenty-five, who acted twice that age. I found out later he was a permanent guest, a policeman in the town. It was he who later brought the news to Mrs Kelly about the first boat to Mull having to turn back because of the weather, and of the second – the one I intended to catch – being delayed indefinitely.

Mrs Kelly related this news to me in a mood of joyful panic. I decided to leave anyway; if the weather calmed there would be a boat in the early afternoon and I could explore the town meanwhile. Mrs Kelly wished me luck, and said she had never been to Mull herself – though it was less than an hour's sailing away – but was hoping to go one day. She said that if the ferry trouble left me high and dry I should not hesitate to come back; she would reserve my half of the bed until teatime.

A boat finally left for Mull at four-thirty in the afternoon, by which time the sea was still as ice.

$$\star \quad \star \quad \star$$

The rain stopped when the wind died down, and then started again without it.

'Just arrived?'

'Yes.'

I was looking at a man in his early twenties, dressed in working clothes, with a fair moustache which looked like it had been stuck on to his upper lip with glue.

'Welcome,' he said, with heavy irony.

'Thanks.'

From Craignure, the north-eastern port of Scotland's next largest island after Skye, I had caught a bus to Bunessan, on the southern part of the Ross of Mull, which points towards Iona. We watched the rain beating straight and hard on the shore road from the window of the hotel bar where he had greeted me. It was dim and cold and the sea we looked on to was grey. The high mountains of Glen More, which the bus had run through, were on the verge of turning purple as the heather came into bloom; by repute magnificent, in this weather they were grimly imposing, and the air of this place increased the unwelcoming effect.

The young man came from Oban and was working here on a building site. He was saving up to get married, worked every night until eight o'clock and restricted himself to one drink a night and a snack in the hotel.

'What brings you to this hell-hole?' he asked.

'I'm looking for someone I've never met.'

Bunessan is a random place. A line of houses rims its main street which curls around the sea front. On a comb of land projecting into the sea on the opposite side of the narrow bay, there are scattered crofts, many of them unworked, and fishermen's cottages.

'Can you tell me where I would find Seaview Cottage?'

He shook his head. 'Where?'

I repeated it. 'Douglas Cameron lives there, a prawn fisherman.'

'Ah, yes. I'll take you there.'

It was about a mile away, on the small promontory which he told me was Ardtun. The young man introduced me to other people who knew my putative host; some lived in other villages, but everyone talked of everyone else with the familiarity of a next-door neighbour, even when they lived thirty miles away, beyond a high mountain, but on the same island.

A few sheep were grazing round the porch of the small cottage when I knocked on the door, and the high tide ventured almost to the back wall of the house. Over the years it had left a thick carpet of stinking brown seaweed outside the back window.

Douglas Cameron came to the door. He had agreed to put me up for a few nights when I called from Oban and introduced myself as a friend of a friend. He was in his thirties, tall and bearded and thin, with the frame and temperament of a hermit; frequently smiling, he was a weary fisherman.

I produced a bottle but he would not drink from it – as he would not eat the fish outside his window – and so I warmed myself while he complained of over-fishing, of foreign boats in his waters, of irresponsible trawling practices whereby immature fish are caught in smaller nets than the law permits. Nowadays, from his small boat, he fished only for prawns and even those, he feared, could soon be exhausted. He showered me with hardship stories, although not from self-pity, and when I asked him to describe the present state of his fishing he would only say: 'It's better than last year but not as good as the year before.' Then he laughed aloud at himself. 'That's what a fisherman always tells people. If you tell them it's lousy, they won't believe you; and of course you can't allow anyone to think you're doing too well, or anything.'

In the morning he would be up and gone early. His working day had a monotonous rhythm: with his partner he sailed to where their creels had been planted the day before, and lifted them on deck by means of a steel rope pulley. The prawns were then unloaded, distinguished by grades, and then the creels were baited with mackerel and sunk in a line once more. This took from very early morning – sometimes four a.m., depending on the tide – until about six in the evening, after which the catch was sorted into boxes and driven in a trailer to a rendezvous point some fifteen miles away.

There, they were picked up by another fisherman, with whom Douglas co-operated and competed simultaneously, and transported to Craignure in time for the first ferry next morning.

He held out small hope for his fishing career and confessed that he had tried, so far in vain, to mortgage his boat.

'There's just nothing down there,' he said.

'What will you do if and when you give it up?'

Douglas shrugged and stood up: it was nine thirty and time for him to go to bed.

'What does everybody else do? Look around you. They join the great tourist chase. Scotland For Sale. In places with no industry of their own you'll find that life is stimulated to feed the tourist hunger. That's where I disagree with the Tourist Board and all those other folk who keep saying you have to stimulate the tourist industry. What about the community? When the people become nothing more than the object of the tourists' curiosity, then the life of the community has had it.'

'Is that what's happening here?'

'It's happening all over the Highlands and Islands, and anywhere with employment problems. It's a backward process, and in Iona it's reached a state of perfection.'

II

The little isle of Earraid lies close in to the south-west corner of the Ross of Mull: the sound of Iona on one side, across which you may see the isle and church of Columba; the open sea to the other, where you shall be able to mark, on a clear, surfy day, the breakers running white of many sunken rocks. I first saw it, or first remember seeing it, framed in the round bull's eye of a cabin port, the sea lying smooth along its shores like the waters of a lake, the colourless, clear light of the early morning making plain its heathery and rocky hummocks. There stood upon it, in these days, a single rude house of uncemented stones, approached by a pier of wreckwood. It must have been very early, for it was then summer, and in summer, in that latitude, day scarcely withdraws; but even at that hour the house was making a sweet smoke of peats which came to me over the bay, and the bare-legged daughters of the cottar were wading by the pier.

I rose to find a brighter morning and the view across the sea transformed. Douglas was already gone, and the cottage was empty. He had left a note for me in the kitchen, inserted into a copy of Robert Louis Stevenson's *Memories and Portraits*, at the page from which the above is taken: an excerpt from the essay, 'Memoirs of an Islet'. On the scrap of paper was written a telephone number and a girl's name.

Until Douglas mentioned it the previous evening, in an effort to dissuade me from going to Iona, it had not occurred to me that Earraid – the islet upon which Stevenson's David Balfour in *Kidnapped* is washed ashore and stranded for several days, surviving on a diet of limpets and buckies – was close by. It is now inhabited by a religious community, and the number which Douglas had passed on to me was their main link with the outside world.

When I telephoned they suggested that I arrive at about one o'clock, at which time, the tide being out, it would be possible to walk across the bed of the sound on to Earraid – something which David Balfour failed to discover, improbably, for four days.

The tidal islet is now owned by two Dutch brothers who lease it to a religious foundation based in Morayshire. The community on Earraid is a changing one, altering rather like a football team, with one or two members being replaced at a time, so that although the composition on the community never remains the same for long, it keeps continuity.

At first, as you approach from the Ross, Earraid looks like a part of Mull, but as you walk towards the houses and the crop of rock behind them, the muddy sea bed from which the water recedes twice a day grows visible. Stevenson's 'single rude house' is long gone, replaced by a neat row of lighthouse-keepers' cottages which his father built in the 1860s while constructing a lighthouse fifteen miles out on the reef of Dhu Heartach, and the pier of wreckwood has been rebuilt into a strong stone structure, which is seldom used now.

The inhabitants were gathered in one of the cottages, preparing lunch and planning a revision of the independent water supply. I left them and clambered over the wall at the back of the 'street' – quaintly numbered one to nine – and climbed the hill, at the top of which Balfour's Bay (or Traigh Gheal, White Sands Bay) where Stevenson played while his father was at work on the lighthouse and where he later had David Balfour come ashore after the brig *Covenant* came to grief on the Torran Rocks, was fully visible.

The present community had sixteen members, seven of them children; most were English – no Scots – and there were two Americans and a Dutchman. The cottages were in a dilapidated condition when the first 'team' arrived, but had been impressively restored, and were sparsely but comfortably furnished. Over lunch they spoke of their efforts to live self-sufficiently, admitting the difficulties involved, and talking as freely about the plans which had failed as those which had succeeded. Since each member had invested a few hundred pounds in the project, their main source of subsidy was themselves.

The longest serving member, Charles, a soft-spoken man who assumed the office of leader, told me of their methods and aims.

'We have a few animals, not many, and large vegetable gardens in front of the houses, where we grow potatoes, carrots, lettuce and anything else we can. Every day, myself and one other person go out and bring in the salmon nets and the lobster creels. Whatever these bring in we sell – the catch is not for eating. We rarely eat meat. Then there are crafts, such as candle-making, and we accept paying guests as well. All together, it creates an island economy, which is not yet self-sufficient, although naturally that's our goal.'

There were certain dependencies on mainland society which they were forced to acknowledge, sometimes by law – for example, the education of their children. Charles and his wife had one child, with another on the way. Another woman member had three children. They spoke disparagingly of the local (Bunessan) school, and said openly that at the slightest excuse they kept the children at home.

'They get no art lessons at all,' said Charles's wife Carol, 'and hardly any heed is paid to many of the things which we regard as important, such as music and dancing. That's the kind of thing I could be teaching them here. So,' she began to laugh, 'on those days when the tide is too rough to make a crossing, I set up a little classroom in here and give them music lessons.'

A conversation I had overheard in the Bunessan shop that morning now became clearer. A woman customer, presumably a parent, had been gossiping to the shopkeeper about the Earraid parents' suspected dislike of the village school. My sympathies were divided and now, before Carol, I kept silent. No one could blame her for wanting the best and most varied education for her son, but keeping him back from the local school implied a disregard, even faint contempt, for the school's other children and their parents. One did not need to be loyal to state educational methods and standards to see how Carol's resistance would cause bewilderment and drive a broader wedge than that which already existed between this private community and the native one on which it was forced to depend, yet wished to reject, and which surely sought any chance to regard these people as just another kind of tourist anyway.

'I think more and more people are finding that the competitive, materialist society out there doesn't satisfy all their needs,' said Charles, 'their deepest needs. I think more and more people will turn away from it and realise that only a certain relationship with nature can give them a lasting basis for their lives. That's what our foundation was established for, and that's why we're here. I'm not saying we're totally successful in all the things we try to do, but all of us keep trying because we've all had experience of that "other" life, out there, and found it wanting.'

After lunch I 'helped', and got a taste of the effort required to satisfy these needs even partially. (Normally, helpers were accepted only as paying guests, at a rate of ninety pounds per week.) With Charles and another man called Rick, I dug potatoes for the evening meal (which was served with a rich, heavy home-made stout), chopped wood, helped Carol to feed and milk the three cows, gathered some hens' eggs, and endured a tiring performance in the rain with Rick in an effort to improve the island's water supply by means of fitting a longer and better hose between the tank and the reservoir. Afterwards, Charles went out to check the nets and creels – the catch was three small lobsters, but no salmon.

At supper, Carol told me about the fortnight she had recently spent on the island of Lewis, where her parents owned some land. She spoke of that second home in a fond tone, which called up pictures of a rural paradise, and contrasted strongly in my mind with my late conversation with Iain Crichton Smith and his bitter tirade against the ministers: 'I feel like *hitting* them in the face . . . It's power they want . . . ' And I sought but failed to find a way to bring the contrast before Carol in a manner which might illuminate it for both of us. But how could she be expected to know anything of his anger? The private lens through which she saw that island, like this, and the very vocabulary in which she spoke of it (and, although I could not say so, the *accent* in which she employed that vocabulary) meant that she was safely sealed off from the mistrust of his spiritual enemies. The island community made no sense to her, she was free of the demands of its history, and therefore was free to confront it, as almost all outsiders confront the whole of the Highlands and Islands, only through its scenic detail. For Crichton Smith, on the other hand, as for many Highlanders, such simplicity belonged, if it had ever existed, to the private domain of childhood. With maturity came deprivation.

'Here they have no time for the fine graces of poetry,' he wrote in 'Poem of Lewis':

> The great forgiving spirit of the word
> fanning its rainbow wing, like a shot bird
> falls from the windy sky. The sea heaves
> in visionless anger over the cramped graves
> and the early daffodil, purer than a soul,
> is gathered into the terrible mouth of the gale.

'We say a prayer for Lewis every night,' Carol said with the laugh I had heard so often throughout the day, pulling her son towards her and hugging him. 'That was a promise I made my parents.'

'Where do they come from?'

'Hampshire.'

'How do they like it in Lewis?'

'It was their retirement present to themselves – oh, they love it.'

What would be her immediate association if someone were to surprise her by mentioning the name of Lewis out of the blue?

'Ancient beauty!'

Later, Charles rowed me out into the sound in the dark. It was fairly rough and there had been a question about whether we could make the crossing or not, but when I said that I would like to get back to Bunessan that night, Charles took me down to the pier, unmoored the small rowing boat and backed towards Mull.

III

Douglas continued to try to change my mind.

'Go down to the road there, and watch the coaches passing every ten minutes, that should put you off if I can't. Every one of them is full and they're all bound for Iona, which is about the size of my back garden.'

I went anyway, crossing at Fionnphort – pronounced '*Finn*afort'. Since I missed the ferry by only a few seconds, I was first in line for the next, which was due a quarter of an hour later. By the time it arrived, the queue at my back was seventy-five yards long.

Iona was originally known as 'Hii'. It was renamed Iova by a fifteenth-century biographer of Saint Columba, which a careless copyist transcribed as Iona. It is, or has been, known also as Icolmkill – the isle of Colum of the Church – Ia, or simply, I, which, given its present dependence on the world's admiration, appeals to the fancy.

Iona is surrounded by names: everything has a name, every bay and reef: Eilean Didel, Eilean Cailbhe, Eilean na h-Aon Chaorach, Carraig an Daimh, Rubh na Carraig geire, Sgeir an Uir, A'Mbachair, Port na Churaich, Carn-Cul-ri-Erin . . . The unpronounceable litany would fill pages, if the name of every point, cave, hillock, beach and lochan were noted. What kind of particularity produced so many names, one wonders, in a place three miles long by one across? Some have a connection with the saint who in 563 AD made Iona the base of his mission to Christianise the Picts: Port na Churaich, 'port of the coracle', for example, refers to the bay where his boat is said to have landed; 'Carn-Cul-ri-Erin, 'cairn of the back turned to Ireland', occurs in a manuscript poem entitled 'Columcille fecit' (although there is nothing to confirm the saint's authorship):

> That I might hear the thunder of the crowding waves
> Upon the rocks;
> That I might hear the roar by the side of the church
> Of the surrounding sea;

That I might see its noble flocks
  Over the watery ocean;
That I might see the sea monsters,
  The greatest of all wonders;
That I might see its ebb and flood
  In their career;
That my mystical name might be, I say,
  Cul ri Erin . . .

It is improbable that the author of this poem actually is Columba, since nothing else on the island except a few names has a direct connection with his arrival here in the middle of the sixth century; the nunnery, the abbey, the ancient graveyards of Christian martyrs, the Celtic crosses, are all medieval or later.

These monuments, which had attracted a thousand visitors today alone, could not arouse my interest, and I walked back on to the boat and left the little island and its dead metaphors.

8

The Colonel Cheats at Frieda

I

'We'll kill something every day, that should keep us happy.'

There was a lovely smell of burning wood in the large drawing room.

The managing director placed his glass of whisky on the edge of the mantelpiece and stooped to rough the shaggy ears of a King Charles spaniel, which responded keenly from its perch on his wife's knees. He lifted his glass again and drank from it, releasing a grave but contented sigh after swallowing, listening expectantly at sounds from the kitchen.

'Refill?'

I drained my glass and gave it up and he walked across to the cabinet and picked up a litre bottle of whisky, from which he carelessly let some splash into both glasses.

'You know,' he said from the corner of the room, in an enquiring tone, 'I sometimes feel there's something quite sort of . . . *mys*tical about shooting. Do you know what I mean?'

I had assumed he was talking to me, since no one else appeared to be listening, but a voice from one of the other small groups stationed around the room protested:

'Edward! That's a terrible thing to say. It's absolutely un-Christian!'

'There's nothing in scripture against stalking,' another voice spoke up in support.

'Even so.'

The managing director returned with my replenished glass and took up his position at the fireplace once again.

'Your very good health. I didn't catch your name.'

'I travel everywhere by car,' his wife, Lady Glengoile, was saying in a resigned manner, pointing at the dog nestling on her lap, 'because I always have . . . ' she reduced her voice to a whisper, '*h-e-r* . . . with me.' She tickled the animal's ears and then fondled them affectionately. 'Don't I, my heart, don't I? Eh?'

Edward, the managing director, Lord Glengoile, sauntered towards the map room, adjacent to the drawing room where ten or twelve people waited patiently while dinner evolved in the kitchen. Three cooks were on duty preparing it. Everyone was hungry, especially those who had been out stalking or shooting in the rain. It had poured all day without respite. I had been out in it too, but not at sport.

By bus I had gone to Mull's port of Craignure, where I took the boat to Oban; then a train ran me to Crianlarich, where I disembarked, since the railway line dipped south at that point, towards Stirling, while my aim was north-west. Rather lost, I had wandered around in the rain until I found someone I could ask about bus services. The answer was simple: no buses ran directly across country.

There was nothing else for it but to hitch-hike once again. It was dim, cold and very wet – all that is contained in the Scots word 'dreich' – but the lifts came surprisingly easily, considering the sight I presented to drivers. I travelled with a doctor from Oban, then an elderly lady from Kingussie, and then with a young farmer's son in a Renault 4, whose back seat had been folded down to hold three large, black-brown, pleasantly smelling Jacob sheep. Near Pitlochry, the car broke down and I had to get out in the rain to push while the driver jump-started and the sheep shifted their position in the back.

Now I was clean and changed, drinking the Colonel's whisky on his fifteen thousand acres in Glennarra, slightly less than a one-hundredth part of the county of Perthshire. It was at first a curious discovery to find myself here after Douglas's leaky, cold cottage by the sea-shore, the result of a casual invitation dealt out months previously.

Edward beckoned to me to follow him into the map room.

'These are ptarmigan.' He indicated two white stuffed birds poised on a slab of wood on top of a tallboy; one was frozen in the act of protecting itself with a wing. Edward sipped his Scotch.

'Aren't they beautiful? Hmm? Look at those feathers – have you ever seen anything so white and delicate as that? You have to go quite high up to get a shot at them, you see? They're there all the year round. Don't come below . . . oh, three thousand feet? Are you staying long? If the weather's picked up tomorrow we might go out and see if we can bag a few, hmm?'

In the drawing room, two of the other guests were engaged in earnest conversation over the dog which stayed close to Lady Glengoile's bosom.

'Isn't she nice? Don't you think she's marvellous, this dog?'

'Oh, wonderful.'

'Amazing. Aren't you, little Busby? Eh?'

'Is that its name, Busby?'

'*Her* name,' interjected Lady Glengoile.

'Oops!'

The large drawing room in the mock Georgian house gave scope for several conversations and activities to be in progress all at once. Each of its windows varied the prospect of the long glen, which even in this weather was spectacular. The bedrooms went into double figures, and at this time of year, during the grouse-shooting, thanks to the Colonel's generosity, its corridors were full.

'This rain will bring out the heather,' someone said.

'Is it time for the heather? I thought it blossomed in the spring.'

'Oh, Paul!'

'Better ask James.'

'Are you *literally* Scotch, James?'

'Don't say Scotch, silly. I said that to poor old Mr Wilkie the other day. He was furious.'

'What does one say then? Scottish?'

'Do they live here all the year round, the Wilkies?'

'"Scots" is in fashion,' I said. 'But any of them will do.'

'There's something I want to ask you, if you are Scottish – or Scots, or even Scotch, for that matter,' said the Colonel's pretty niece who was hanging up pictures in a corner near the map room. 'One of the gillies said something yesterday, what was it now? – Oh yes, "glaikit", what does that mean? "He's offy glaikit", or something, was what he said.'

The others shrieked at her deadpan impersonation.

'I didn't like to ask.'

I said it meant stupid.

'Oh, how clever of you.'

'You're going to be literally snowed under with questions if you admit to being Scottish, James.'

'Isn't it funny, though, how words change their meanings,' Edward remarked.

'Yes, but that isn't one that's changed, it's just a Scottishism.'

'But all the same. You listen to the BBC, for example –'

'Oh, the BBC's *dread*ful!' said the niece.

'You'll hear all sorts of words pronounced the wrong way, when they read the news and so on. Have you noticed? I mean, *re*-search, for example, for re-*search*; and *ro*-mance –'

'One that really gets my goat is *dis*-pute, for dispute.'

'Americanisms are killing the language stone dead,' said Edward.

'How do you pronounce the names of all those islands?' asked the niece. 'I-s-l-a-y, for example?'

'Islay.'

'And J-u-r-a. I suppose that's just Jura.'

'Very good stalking on Jura,' said Edward.

She returned to hanging pictures. All round the walls already there were prints and paintings of different species of bird – including ptarmigan – mostly captured by the artist at the moment of being shot; there were pictures of deer and of men shooting at deer, and of dogs leaping at their necks; of fish apparently suspended in mid-air, fish laid out on a silver platter, fish on a fishmonger's slab, and newly caught fish being watched over by a dog who looked very like Busby.

Dinner was announced at last, by which time all the guests had assembled in the drawing room, including the Colonel and the Colonel's wife, dressed in evening clothes. Lord and Lady Glengoile's teenage son arrived and was allowed a vermouth on condition that it be well topped with lemonade. He was thin and fresh-faced with a permanent smirk.

'We got one at last,' he boasted to his great-aunt, the Colonel's wife.

'Oh, you mean a stag! How wonderful – your first! Simon's got his first stag, everybody!'

'Did you have to have your face dipped in blood and everything?' asked the niece.

Simon said he did and there was general applause, in the middle of which Busby grew excited and began barking loudly.

★   ★   ★

That evening, after dinner, everyone played a game called frieda in the billiards room. It involves just a red ball and a white ball and as many players as desired, and is played in rota according to standing positions round the billiard table. The red ball must remain in motion, and each player has to hit it by propelling the white ball manually, from either end of the table. Everyone starts with three lives and if you miss, a life is lost. It is more difficult than it sounds, and the lives drop away quickly.

The Colonel, a sturdy man of seventy, won the first game, battling out a final with his nephew William. Then we played again. The same two finalists were left after everyone else had forfeited three lives, and once again the Colonel triumphed.

Afterwards, Lord Glengoile remarked to William that it was wonderful that the old man could still run rings round the lot of us.

'He cheated,' said William, without rancour.

★   ★   ★

The Colonel lined his sights on a thrush in a nearby tree.

'Ever shot anything?'

I had to admit, with slight regret, that I had not, and so Edward, handing out the guns before the house in the morning, was obliged to pass me by.

They were hung on a rack in the rear of the Land Rover, and then our small convoy set off through the treeless glen. I thought the journey would never end, as we left the paved road and started on a narrower, rutted track, progressing by dint of a series of shocks.

'It's amazing,' Edward remarked. 'Friends of ours from Surrey have a house at the top of Glen Lyon, which is a continuation of this one, and if you kept walking for about thirty miles you would eventually reach their house. Between them and us there isn't a single permanent resident. Isn't that wonderful?'

'Makes you think, doesn't it?' said William from the front seat.

The Colonel himself was driving. This was a big day for him, only the third or fourth time he had been to his estate to go shooting this year. Because of his age, he visited the estate less often, and the husbandry and general management were left mainly to William, although having his permanent home in London, he was even further from Scotland for most of the year than the Colonel, who lived in Derbyshire. It was agreed, by and large, that William was making a decent job of it, although tax and duties were a constant worry. So far, they had not resorted to the practice common on other estates, including the neighbouring one at Glen Lyon, of renting out rooms of the house to sportsmen in search of a week's shooting, though it was reassuring to have the option of doing so if things got rough. Some businessmen, I heard it said, will fly from the United States for a single day's shooting on such game reserves.

Finally, we reached our destination and the Colonel produced a small leather pouch from which the men drew lots for shooting positions, then we fanned out in a line accordingly. A taciturn gillie (the only Scotsman I had seen in three days) kept his eye on the line, as the manoeuvre began.

There was the slightest nervous anticipation about our line as we advanced. Every so often the cry of 'Go back!' came from the gillie. The tension did not lift until the first covey swept into the air: six or seven grouse took off away from us before wheeling round on the wind as if to sail above our heads. By the time the gillie shouted 'Edward!' the gun was at his shoulder, but the shot thudded and missed. The Colonel, waiting for him, fired immediately afterwards and a bird dived groundwards, as if coming in to land.

The gillie's setter paced towards it and picked it up – the bird's wings were still fluttering as he ran back towards us with it in his mouth. The Colonel accepted it, looked it over, and then tossed it to his gillie, who thumped its neck once or twice with his stick before stuffing the body, still twitching, into his shoulder bag.

Sometimes a bird was winged and did not fall immediately but flew on until it reached a rock or some other resting place. When this happened, the dogs were sent after it, and if that failed then whoever fired the shot would go and try to find and finish off his prey, as much out of respect for the enemy as from a desire to increase the toll.

We marched five or six miles in this way, halting when a brace or more rose from the heather, firing, and then continuing. When eventually we sat down and rested, the count was low – seven and a half brace – the result of a bad season, not of the standard of marksmanship, which was high. The Colonel himself, Edward said, would have once expected to take about fifteen brace in a day. The complaint about a scarcity of game was uttered often in my presence; although it seemed, rather obviously, to negate the favourite argument in defence of hunting and shooting – that numbers have to be kept down – that too was spoken frequently, with never a thought for the contradiction it offered.

On the way back a hare leapt from a tussock and darted away from our advancing line. Hares are difficult to shoot because of their speed, and one or two had already rocketed before us. This time the Colonel almost trod on it before it started out: he was too surprised to do anything but exclaim in surprise, but Edward had his gun to his shoulder in a second and a split second later the hare was ready to join the grouse in the bag.

★　　★　　★

After dinner that evening, about fifteen people played at frieda. Lady Glengoile seemed desperate to perform well; she took off her high-heeled shoes and dashed round the table when her turn came, long arms and legs shooting this way and that and an evening dress of bottle green flashing as she moved in and out of the billiard table light. Everyone cheered as she flung herself half across the table to grab the red ball and make one of her wild tosses in the direction of the white.

'Hip, hip!'

'Oh, *wond*-erful!'

But eventually, and in spite of protests and sympathetic cries of

'Shame!', her third life passed and she was out, and this time it was I who reached the final after everyone but the Colonel had forfeited three lives . . . and again he won.

II

I know this very large county intimately. Looking over the 1874 record I was struck by the size of the Breadalbane estate – 233,200 acres (£36,000) in Perthshire, continuing into Argyll with another 204,200 acres (£22,300) – a total of 437,000 acres with an annual return of £60,000. This huge Campbell estate appears to have grown up during the eighteenth and nineteenth centuries, flourished until around 1900, and then rapidly disappeared, so the present Earl, who lives in Hampstead, now owns no land of any consequence. The same feature occurs with the neighbouring family of Menzies – 116,000 acres a century ago, and none today. Why this happened does not, I think, matter very much. My point, and this is one of the terrible features of land-ownership not only in Perthshire but all over Scotland, is that our most precious asset can be played about with in some gambling den, or as a result of family feuds, with the consequence that the land is abused and the rural communities perish.

The one huge remaining estate, Atholl, had 194,000 acres (£36,000) in 1874. It still covers 130,000 acres. Drummond Castle estate has shrunk from 76,800 acres to 65,000, and Charles Drummond-Moray's estate at Abercairney from 40,600 acres to 13,000 acres. Another Murray (one more of 'the very-well-able-to-look-after-themselves' clan) has Scone Palace. In 1874 this estate was 31,197 acres in size with the very high annual value of £23,000, but the present owner, Lord Mansfield, has increased his holdings to 33,800 acres, all of it on high quality land. Lord Mansfield is as well known as his Chief, the Duke, but he lays no claim to owning deer forests, though his father and he have been leaders in blood sports in Scotland.

The same acquisitive attitude could be credited to the Stuart Fotheringhams of Grandtully and Murthly who, in 1874, owned 33,300 acres and have now amassed just on 45,000 acres. About 15,000 acres of it is let to an American syndicate as a game reserve, to which sportsmen from the US fly, even for a single day's shoot. This is another example of the contemptible ways in which our Scottish landlords treat our land.

The 12,000 acre estate at Dupplin, held in 1874 by the Earl of Kinnoull, has been taken over by Lord Forteviot (Dewar's Whisky). These 12,000 acres are about the most fertile in Scotland and Lord Forteviot knew what he was doing. I gather its agricultural section is well managed, but in forestry the good lord has a lot to learn. In 1874 the Duke of Montrose had 32,000 acres, but now none, and the Earl of Moray, whose ancestors seem to have prowled a lot, now owns 10,800 acres, reduced from 40,600.

It is extremely difficult to trace what has happened to the huge areas once owned by Campbell of Breadalbane and the Menzies. Certainly the Wills family estates in Glen Lyon and Rannoch have grown to a total of 70,000 acres. Meggernie estate in Glen Lyon is the site of one of Perthshire's biggest scandals, where agriculture and forestry is sacrificed for game.

John McEwen,
from 'Perthshire',
Who Owns Scotland (1981 edition)

★   ★   ★

The family which owns Glennarra has no connection with the nation which contains it, not even the remote historical link which is frequently invoked to justify possession of wide acres of beautiful, depopulated, profitable Scotland. They make some simple attempts to participate in local customs – the Colonel, for example, wears a kilt on gala occasions, such as the local Highland Games, if he happens to be on his estate at the time – and some efforts are made to accommodate certain of the immediate community's expectations, such as attendance at church on Sunday mornings, where William and his wife were considering having their new-born baby daughter christened, possibly with a Scots middle name, such as Catriona or Fionna, although the matter was unresolved by the time of my departure.

As was another, more serious business: William's efforts to become the prospective Conservative candidate for the constituency of Perth and Kinross in time for the next election. The sitting MP, although popular enough to have kept his seat for many years, had had his future complicated by some domestic turbulence, and William was hoping to capitalise. In the end, however, he failed to do so, and began seeking a candidacy in England.

Had he been elected as member for Perth and Kinross, William would have had the task of representing farmer Tom Gray, who lives south of Glennarra in this large county. It is doubtful if Tom

Gray would have placed much faith in William's ability, or desire, to improve his lot, even though ostensibly the aspiring Tory candidate ought to have rejoiced in Tom Gray's personal endeavour.

I went to visit him after a chance meeting in a pub on Sherrifmuir, near a small village where I had come to pay a brief visit to some relations. Getting to Tom's place was difficult. I had to go at night, since he could not take time off to see me during the hours of light, and needed to borrow a car to get there. I drove past a series of landmarks which he had described to me, until I came in sight of a long, low caravan perched on the hump of a hill, with two yellow squares on its side burning through the dark. Next to the caravan was a large building with a steeply sloping roof, which looked to be in a half-finished state. Tom had said earlier in the day that he intended to build his own house, and for a second I assumed this was it. However, I soon discovered that it was only the barn; with his wife and two children, Tom lived in the caravan.

The hum of the electricity generator disturbed the air outside the car. The windmill which he intended to erect to supply his house and farm with energy had not yet been passed by the authorities, leaving him dependent on a generator. 'Authorities' of all kinds, indeed, were the bane of his life, and prominent among them were the owners of the 136 acres which he and his father farm and which has been in the family for forty years. In that time, the land had changed hands more than once, each time making the working tenants feel less secure. The latest 'lairds' were Arabs, whom Tom had never seen, far less met, except once when he spotted a limousine driving round the estate and assumed it must be theirs. All his negotiations take place through the medium of the factor.

The traditional view of the laird-factor-tenant string is that the kindness of the man at the top prepares the one at the bottom for the rough handling from the middle-man. To put it another way, the laird can afford his geniality because the factor does all the dirty work. There are fewer factors on estates now but in rural areas, where the laird is often popular, the traditional view prevails and factors are commonly disliked.

'They want us off this land,' Tom Gray told me when I was inside his eight-by-ten-foot living room, where his two daughters were watching television and his wife busied herself with household tasks, occasionally confirming or rebutting his strong opinions. 'That's all there is to it. The factor came to my father one day – he was just going about his normal day's work on the farm – and said, "Mr Gray, there's no future for your sons here after you die." Just like that. Are you surprised I'm sour? We're still here, though. We're not dead yet.'

'Though it's surprising,' said Mrs Gray.

Earlier in the day I had seen the farmhouse where his elderly parents had lived since beginning to work the farm. It was a pleasant, remote place, but inside the wallpaper hung from the damp brown walls. 'I don't think they can last for another winter,' Tom had said.

His soreness is aggravated by the fact that six years ago he almost succeeded in purchasing fifty-six acres of land from a farmer who was, as he said, well disposed towards the little man, but as a result of confusion over the terms of purchase finally sold the land to someone else. The lucky buyer's first act was to build a large house on his new land – I had passed it on my drive up to the caravan – it was still as empty as the day the door was first locked.

'When this land here which Father and I work changed hands from the old owners to the new ones, the first we learned of it was when we got a letter through the post. We've never once been offered the opportunity to buy the place ourselves. All we get the chance to do – and even that is slipping away – is work it day after day. People tell me I'm a radical for urging the government towards some kind of land reform – but what's radical about that? It would be for the good of everyone, after all, if more land was utilised. But because its value appreciates so quickly, the land is the only thing the landowners are interested in. We're just a pest as far as they're concerned. Why do you think they're so remiss when it comes to making repairs in Father's house? They want us out all right. The rent from a small farm like this is of no concern to them . . . And the new owners, who have only bought the land for its money value, think of the tenants as an even bigger nuisance than the previous owners did, since they were used to them.

'Renting a farm under these conditions is not good for the moral fibre of a family – neither for the tenant nor the landlord, come to that. If the farm, and the land it stands on, belongs to the farmer, then he has an interest in it – he looks after it and improves it. But the way it is here, anything you've done to the land becomes theirs when you finally move off. It's not surprising, then, that they've found that the land gets better farmed when *we* do it than when they do it themselves.

'One of the most poignant things about farms is that you can always tell, even as you're just passing on the road, which category it falls into – whether it's farmed by an absentee landlord, whether it's tenanted, or whether it's an owner-occupied farm. The first type usually have empty buildings and cottages all over the place, and a general unlived-in look about them – maybe there's nothing in the yard except a couple of cars or something like that. On the tenanted farm, the buildings are usually second-rate, a lot of repairs needing done, there's likely to be no tarmac, any recent construction looks as if it's not built to last, and so on. Whereas, in the last category – well, it's just as it is with a house: this is their lot, their investment. They keep it spruce, and when they have any improvements to make they do them properly. These farms often have a look of prosperity about them which the other two kinds don't have.'

'Do people ever accuse you of having a chip on your shoulder?'

Mrs Gray laughed suddenly. 'Everyone!'

'If I have, it's for a good reason, is it not? All the subsidies favour the "speculator farmer". The big get bigger, all the time. Ever since the factor said to my father, "There's no future for your sons here", I've been non-conformist, anti-establishment, call it what you like. I do my own thing now. All I want is the resources to farm my own plot of land to the best of my abilities, a place big enough to sustain a family and build a home for us to live in. It doesn't sound like a lot to ask – I'm willing to pay for it – when you've got guys all over the Highlands with more land than they can *count*, and it's doing nothing. I would like to see a government-run national body renting out medium-sized plots to graduate farmers, such as myself.'

'Will you move into your parents' house if you're still here when they die?'

'Why move into a condemned house?'

I left. The good weather had passed for the year now, it seemed certain, and hard drops of rain hit the roof of the car as I drove back along the dark road. There was no moon. I looked out for the untenanted house we had talked about, but missed it in the dark.

9
That Cursed Country

Nearby is a Gaelic college of education. The language issue is important, he says. When their language and culture are stamped out . . . people lose heart and direction. 'I think you'll find that wherever in the world this happens, the people concerned are regarded as lazy and given to drink by their neighbours.'

Guardian
13 November 1982

I

I caught a train at Gleneagles and travelled with it as far as Kingussie, where I lodged overnight, afterwards tracing a zig-zag path by road to Kyle of Lochalsh, where I knew I could meet up with another railway line.

It was north again. From Farmer Gray's I had at first intended to make for Glasgow, but finally could not resist one more incursion into the paradox of the Highlands. This time I stuck to the ragged line of the west coast.

I got lifts with ease: from a cool Anglo-Swedish woman; then a sprightly, youthful granny who drove me recklessly to Glenshiel, a wild spot; and last from a van driver who hardly spoke, apologising for being hooked on radio drama.

★   ★   ★

Lorna was about twenty-five, though she gigglingly refused to admit her age when asked. She had big eyes and a wide mouth, her hair was gathered in a high ponytail, and she held herself with both arms and drew in breath, shivering minutely in her sky-blue polo-neck, and woefully chided the inhospitable Highland climate.

I met her in a hotel in the afternoon. It was a place famous for its situation, settled above the shingle of the lochshore, windows greeting every sunrise across the water. She acted like she owned it, but in fact it belonged to her parents-in-law, who had recently retired, leaving the running of the place in the hands of Lorna and their son.

The occasional flat vowel or trundled 'r' was audible in Lorna's speech; after two years of struggling with Highland voices her own Yorkshire accent was so faint that, had she not immediately impressed the fact of her origins upon me, I might have mistaken hers for a polite Edinburgh voice.

'What do you think of the Highlander?'

I gave some non-committal, tame reply and turned the question round.

'I wouldn't like to tell you,' she said.

'Why not?'

'It would be too rude.'

'You can say anything to me.'

'Well, I think he's a drunken bum. So there. Does that shock you? It's an opinion formed from observation, I can assure you.'

An elderly man and woman, guests in the hotel, strolled past the reception desk on their way out, exchanging pleasantries with Lorna as they went.

'Going fishing?' she asked them.

'We were meant to – but it's too wet.'

'Shame!'

As she returned to face me again, her mouth deposited the smile it had picked up to greet the guests.

'I'm not talking about the ones who've gone off and made something of themselves in the world, It's the ones they've left behind I'm thinking of. They do nothing. They're quite useless for anything except drinking. They live for drink. No, I take that back; two things: drinking and poaching. They work crofts, which they do very badly, and then when they don't make enough money from the croft they draw the dole at the same time. Then they drink the lot of it – all the money they can get their hands on goes on drink. They give their wives nothing at the end of the day, and hit them if they ask for anything.'

'You're a woman of strong opinions, Lorna.'

'They're nothing but a lot of greedy, grasping, bone-idle, good-for-nothing so-and-sos.'

'Do you have any friends among the locals?'

'I wouldn't *have* any of them for my friends. They're unreliable, you can't trust them. They come into the bar here and get absolutely sozzled every night. They'd drink all through the night if you let them. Sometimes we *do* let them. Then, of course, they don't go to work in the morning – if they have jobs, that is. They're just like animals, some of them. No, on second thoughts, I take that back. I don't want to be unkind. I *like* animals.'

'Surely you can find *something* good to say about them.'

'Oh well, I mean they'll give you a lift if you're stuck, or anything like that. For example, if you happen to mention in the bar one evening that you're looking for a lift to Inverness or something, then someone will fix it up for you, just like that. But they'd stab you in the back next time if they got the chance.'

'What experience have you had of that?'

'Me? None. But they would if you let them. I don't allow anyone to get that close to me.'

Her husband came through the glass door into reception, led by a massive Irish wolfhound on a chain. Lorna greeted the dog in baby talk. The husband looked impatient. Tall and thin and dull-looking, he placed his hands on his hips and made a noise I couldn't interpret but which made me want to leave. He thought he had made a good catch in Lorna. Her intuition brought her to explain that I was only pausing out of the rain on my way to Applecross. He nodded gruffly but seemed satisfied and they began to talk about the price of admission to be charged for a buffet-dance being held in the bar some time during the following week. Lorna scorned her husband's estimate as being too low.

'I've heard a few of the lads complain that five pounds would be too high.'

'They're taking advantage of you, Andrew. They think you're soft.'

'Some of them are my friends.'

'Friends! You're in *business*, Andrew!'

He sighed, and in the moment's silence I moved towards the door. Andrew saw it as a way of relieving the tension.

'Have you been to Applecross before?'

'No.'

'It's rather remote. There's a fantastic road leading into the village, though. The steepest gradient in Britain, you know, and only two feet short of being the highest road. That's somewhere in Wales, I believe. What kind of car have you got?'

'I'm hoping for a lift.'

'Oh.' He seemed disappointed in me. 'Well let me give you some advice: make sure that the person you travel with is sober – that road's bloody frightening as it is.'

I went outside, though it was still raining, and stood under a tree by the side of the road. It was closing time and the hotel bar was emptying. A van coming from the car park stopped. The driver said he was only going a few miles but to come on in anyway.

★   ★   ★

Most places have two distinct personalities, one flourishing under sunshine, the other surfacing during rainy dull days. At a glance, a Highland village may appear as the most beautiful, peaceful haven you will ever see; or else as the dreariest incarnation of boredom on earth.

I caught Applecross acting out the second role, and at first most things about it were consistent with my impression.

The only thing the highest gradient in Britain meant to me was fear – halfway to the top we ran into a fog which eventually became so dense that neither I nor the driver could see more than a few yards ahead. Two scrawny red deer leapt in front of us, bringing a screech of brakes from the car and a casual glance backwards from one of them.

When we arrived, the driver let me off in front of the hotel. The main street – the only street – was a string of houses swaddled in mist and drizzle in the shadow of surrounding hills. A once-large fishing fleet has been reduced to one boat, and the population of three thousand last century to a few hundred today.

The hotel did not accept paying guests. I was directed towards two bed and breakfast houses, but neither would take me in. 'No singles,' said Mrs Macall. 'Try Mrs Mackay.' I knocked on her door. 'Try Mrs Macall,' she said.

It was a small street and only by walking on to the adjoining village in the fine rain – a rain which Scots describe as 'very wet' – did I find a place willing to accept me. I was grateful for that but it was a shabby house, set upon a ridge, which made me think of a Glasgow council house uplifted from its place and then dropped from the sky on to the lochshore. The carpet was threadbare, the room character-less; the sheets, I felt sure, had been slept in before. Breakfast in the morning consisted of two strands of salty bacon and an egg.

I had heard so much about this little place, which those who had been here usually claimed as being the remotest they had found, that I could not hide my disappointment from myself, though I knew that its appearance was an effect of the weather rather than the place it rained on or the people who lived there.

Later, I went into the bar of the hotel (the designation must have been kept to satisfy a licensing law), the only possible meeting place. Heavy drinking was compulsory. I watched men drink four pints in the time it took me to finish one. Silence was called at one point to allow a television programme to be heard. When conversation started up again it was good humoured and involved everyone in the bar. People used my first name as if they had known me for a year and seemed as eager to hear tales of the faraway world as I was to savour their remoteness.

The writer to whom Applecross was assigned during the compila-tion of the first *Statistical Account of Scotland* in the late eighteenth century would have agreed in principle with Lorna on at least one point, though his tone was more delicate; the people's behaviour in this parish, he wrote in 1779, is in most ways respectable, but 'the use of spiritous liquors is rather too prevalent'. (He wasn't the only one who thought so, about the country in general, which comes as little surprise when it is considered that in the earlier half of the century the major commodity import to Scotland was French wine and brandy. A traveller to Edinburgh in 1705 recalled that having been warned by everyone he met not to venture into the 'most barb'rous Country in the world', he was astonished to be provided at the first inn he stopped at with 'excellent French white wine and brandy'. A later change in excise duty stemmed the flow of wine, but not the habit of drinking it.)

The *Third Statistical Account*, written and published in the 1950s, continues the style of summarising the habits and character of people and places which is to be found in Sir John Sinclair's original, and also in the *New Statistical Account*, but it occurred to me as I wandered back in the extended gloaming that thumbnail sketches with phrases like 'the people are industrious . . . ', or, 'they are in the habit of hanging out their clothes to dry on the shore . . . ', are not only presumptuous but almost impossible to arrive at today, when television and the motor car have come between the people and their past, between the land and its traditions, bestowing the surface homogeneity which the twentieth century pretends to loathe but continues to demand. In small villages in remote parts of the 'last great European wilderness', the people's songs are Tin Pan Alley, like the people of London or Llandudno, and their favourite diversion is Coronation Street.

II

A recent book for six to ten year olds published by a leading London publisher on 'Great Britain' is not untypical of the material available. Scarcely three pages were devoted to Scotland which was divided into Highlands and Lowlands. No areas of population were shown in the Highlands as 'very few people live there'.

Letter to the *Scotsman*
26 October 1982

My map, which had often been my main reading material, deceived me at last. The high road from Lochcarron to Applecross is no longer the latter's main link with the outside world; a newly built road, wound round the strangely unindented coastline leading to Shieldaig, opened in 1976, but the map which I had with me did not show it – instead, it gave only a footpath, indicated by a thin, broken black line. Furthermore, nothing on the map hinted at the true condition of the villages on the coast, whose names were given for all the world as if they really existed: Lonbain, Kalnakill, Cuaig, Fearnmore, Kenmore, Ardheslaig. . . . Only Shieldaig, the point of destination, safely in view of 'the outside world', is complete.

I set out to walk along the road to the first of them. I read in the newspaper next day that it had been sunny almost everywhere else in the country; here it was grey and misty, with rain always on the approach from the peaks of the Cuillins of Skye, which could be seen from the road across the Sound of Raasay.

Lonbain, eight miles from Applecross, was totally derelict except for one house: a standard Highland blackhouse with windowless dry-stone walling, peat gables and thatch held in place over the roof by bricks suspended from wire; docken leaves and all manner of weeds sprouted from it and from inside came the smell of burning peats.

I found its inhabitant, an old man called Duncan Mackenzie, huddling for shelter at the wall of one of the broken-down out-buildings. He wanted to know the price of things and asked for what I was carrying to be given him as a present. He was born, he told me, in 1904 and had lived in Lonbain all his life, though its other inhabitants left – most of them for New Zealand – 'thirty or forty years ago'. He had the company of a small businessman who worked from a modern house nearby, and of tourists who had heard of his isolation and wanted to sample it for themselves. A film crew had recently used Lonbain as the backdrop for a nostalgic film. A wooden sign tied to the wall of his house stated: 'No Pictures'.

Duncan occupied himself by cutting peats and looking over to Raasay. He was not pleased about the new road which brought cars and their curious owners to look at him and try to photograph his monument of a house. He never left the 'village', he said, because he didn't like crowds. Then he said:

'I hear they're putting eight pence on a gallon of petrol.'

Surprised, I asked him how he knew.

'I heard it on my wireless.'

. ★   ★   ★

Eviction, depopulation, dereliction, dilapidation, wasteland, wilderness . . .

What relation does the meaning of these words and others which are spoken and heard so often in the Highlands, bear to its famous scenic beauty? For the one is inextricably linked to the other, and to consider them apart is merely to shelter in the comfort of an illusion – in this case, of a kind of rural paradise, to which (as is usually so in such divine places) the natives do not subscribe.

Loss of language, loss of literature, loss of music, loss of clothing, economy, law . . . Even in lowland Scotland, sympathy for the destruction of Celtic society is limited to a few students and hobbyists. The people, as Iain Crichton Smith has written, are colonised internally, having been brought up on a diet of foreign education and mass media.

The perfectly obvious assertion that rural people need the land undermines the hope invested in imposed industries such as oil exploration and electronics manufacture – welcome though they no doubt are to those without jobs – which suffer from the same disadvantages as any other outsider. The people take what they can get from them and then leave them alone, if the reverse does not happen first; and the talk of new blood, new life, withers and takes its place among the decrepit adjectives and nouns.

★   ★   ★

I went on to Poolewe, then Gairloch, and then Inverness. The man who took me there was a sailor on leave. He stopped his car and I got in. I smelled immediately what he had been doing since hitting dry land.

'I'm full o' booze!' he said with forced jollity, throwing up his hands from the steering wheel. 'I've been boozin' all day, but what the hell!'

What the hell. I decided to risk it for a mile or two, and then, if necessary, find a reason for wanting to travel some more of the road from Gairloch on foot. But he drove quite slowly and with due care, only once running two wheels on to the grass verge. He was telling me a funny story at the time, about his pre-sailing days as an undertaker, how they once lost a hearse which had a coffin inside, which had a body inside. A new package, filled with earth and stones, was improvised hastily, in time for the funeral, and the undertakers stood with hats off as mourners paid their last respects and the coffin was lowered into the grave. Fortunately, he said, the original coffin never turned up.

★　★　★

It was a mild night in Inverness, perhaps the last mild night of the year this far north. In the morning I went to Culloden Moor, where the last battle on British soil took place in 1746, between Jacobite forces led by Charles Edward Stuart, 'the Young Pretender', and the Hanoverian army of the Duke of Cumberland, who lives on in Highland memory under the name of 'Butcher'. The outcome of the battle put an end to Bonnie Prince Charlie's aspirations to the throne, and marked the beginning of the end for Highland society.

The Battle of Culloden – or Drummossie, as it is sometimes called – lasted under an hour. The preliminary cannonading began just after one o'clock and by two it was all over; one thousand Jacobite soldiers were killed in battle and two hundred more were dragged back and slain on the field before the 'pacification' of the Highlands began: a message sent by fire and sword 'to extirpate the inhabitants of that cursed country'.

10

Frozen Violence

I

The timetable in Inverness railway station promised a train to Glasgow in the afternoon. I deposited my bag in a left-luggage locker and went in search of lunch.

From the other side of the street, the little restaurant looked inviting, but I opened the door and was met by the puerile chatter of a disc jockey introducing empty music. Only lack of time stopped me from turning back. I seated myself in the one corner without a loudspeaker and made a choice from the menu. After about five minutes, the waitress, no older than a schoolgirl, arrived and held up her notepad and pencil.

'Right.'

'What's the chef's special?'

'Roast beef, roast potatoes and peas.'

'Fine. I'll have that.'

'It's finished.'

'Ah...' I quickly considered the menu again. 'Is the pizza your own?'

'No.'

'Well, in that case I'll have the steak.'

She scribbled on her pad.

'And a cup of tea right away, please.'

She turned without saying anything further, and disappeared. Five minutes later I succeeded in catching her eye again.

'What is it?'

'I asked for the tea straight away. I'm thirsty. Could I have it now, please?'

She turned away again, but still the tea did not come. Eventually, she came back with a plate which she placed on my table.

'This is pizza!'

'That's what you wanted.'

'I didn't ask for pizza. I asked for steak.'

She looked at me unbelievingly for a few moments before going to retrieve the plate. I stayed her hand.

'I'll have this anyway. But please bring my tea now. And a napkin.'

Again she disappeared, and I started eating the pizza. It was burnt on the underside, where it had obviously been heated on a hot plate. The waitress came back with my cup of tea.

'What about a napkin?'

She nodded silently and seemed to be going to fetch one. I debated inwardly over whether to complain about the burned pizza, but persevered for a few more mouthfuls. There was still no sign of a napkin and so I stood up and took one myself from a glass tumbler on the counter. When I was back at my table the waitress arrived with another one.

'You've *got* a napkin!' she exclaimed angrily.

'I got it myself. And this pizza's burnt.'

'It's what?'

'Burnt.'

'It's taken you a long time to find out.'

This was true: I had eaten half of it.

'That doesn't alter the fact that it's burnt.'

'Well . . . ' She put her hands on her hips.

'Don't bother. Just give me the bill.'

She scribbled on her notebook, then handed the piece of paper to me.

'Service is included.'

★　★　★

'How long does the journey take?'

To get from Inverness to Glasgow, I guessed, would require just over four hours.

The middle-aged man sitting opposite me in the non-smoking compartment nodded his head cheerfully. He continued to peer out from behind his spectacles, however, without a sign of having been enlightened or even of being interested in what I had said. Around him hung a certain air, which I was now able to intuit at a distance, of wanting to talk.

A month ago, even a week, or perhaps just on a different morning, I would have accommodated him gladly – or even have instigated the conversation myself. But now I was feeling tired – of trains and of waiting for trains and of being told there were no trains; of waiting for lifts in remote places; of too early breakfasts, and of being at the mercy of others' service or favour every hour of every day. And with tiredness had come boredom and irritation. I had been living out of a suitcase for weeks on end, had been deprived, for months, of a familiar room, stocked with familiar possessions, with familiar faces outside the door. Moreover, I had an unshakeable itch to be heading not for Glasgow, but Edinburgh, where the International Festival of the Arts had begun.

The newspaper was filled with Festival news and gossip. I glanced through it, then left it on the table which separated me from my travelling companion, and he instantly picked it up and looked across at me expectantly.

'Of course,' I said, glad to have warded him off. But he read no more than a few paragraphs before insisting that I share his amusement at some story or other.

'This'll make you laugh,' he said, shaking his head.

'I'm sure.'

He tossed the paper back across the table to me and leaned over to point out the item he meant me to read.

The American style 'Casey Jones' fast food take away opens at Glasgow Central Station soon, with the claim that the Scottish public will prefer the fast food concept to the 'traditional cafeteria style queue along the counter rail', according to *Railnews*, the British Rail journal.

Mr Chris Maguire, the Scottish region catering manager, says that by eliminating the possibility of human error they can ensure cooking perfection. Every customer would get the same high-quality product with no variation, thanks to computer-controlled cooking of burger and chips.

'Makes you laugh, eh?'

'In a way.'

Then he said he was going to the buffet and offered to fetch me anything I wanted. I thanked him but declined. He left his seat and returned after a minute with a cup covered by a plastic top, which he removed to sip a little of the steaming liquid.

'It's either tea or coffee,' he said. 'You get a free railcard if you can tell the difference.'

II

An unseasonal wind carried the rain across Eglinton Street and Gorbals Street and Crown Street: parallel lines veering south through the Gorbals to politer suburbs. These unhoused streets have the capacity to disorient the most experienced prowler. Rocky stretches run between streets, now and then interrupted by survivors – a string of houses, lingering hosiery or confectioners' shops, the post office, pre-war cinemas converted into bingo halls. Scrap merchants and car mechanics nestle beneath the railway arches. Skyscrapers with ironic- sounding names stem from level platforms on ground which is elsewhere uneven.

I grew up in Glasgow, attended school and first went out to work here. My deepest memories are Glaswegian, and I have difficulty separating these from present responses to the city. Examining my feelings, I find myself measuring them out in contradictions: of love and fear, admiration and revulsion, pride and despair; above all the sense that it belongs to me.

If I try to look at it like a foreigner I see, in the centre, the destruction of a secure pattern of streets and shops to make way for ugly real-estate, and in the suburbs rude backsides of brown tenements and patchy wastelands with ghosts of dwellings. Over all, the sky like a slate.

Yet I know that there are several Glasgows: it is the city that proves better than any other that people make places. There is the notorious violence of the slums, and the city divided by sectarian hatred; the Victorian Glasgow beloved by architecture enthusiasts; the 'friendliest city in the world'; the Glasgow of music hall and street comedians; and many others. For the people own it. At every level of discourse, from official histories to common speech, its citizens confidently proclaim their common ownership of all amenities and monuments. Glasgow will not tolerate pretentiousness or hypocrisy for long; people expect the people they meet to be ordinary. The man at the bus stop who informs you of his shop steward's virtues or failings expects, without question, that you have a shop steward to complain about too. The man on his way to the betting shop who asks 'Who won the three thirty?' takes it for granted not only that you will know what 'the three thirty' stands for, but that you knew it was being run.

The reasons why Glaswegians possess this sense of community in greater degree than citizens of most other cities are related to what was until recently the cornerstone of Glasgow life: the tenement, a four or five-storey walk-up building with two or three flats on each floor, possessing a common toilet, stairway and close. In a street of tenements, one extended family sometimes occupied most of a single close, or else was scattered about the neighbouring ones, so that the pattern of living often resembled that of a village. Doors would be left open in daytime, inviting unexpected callers, and no one was allowed to cross the threshold in such a house without being offered food and drink. The unkind Scottish joke, 'You'll have had your tea?' does not originate here.

The majority of tenements have been swept away in the latest programme of slum clearance. Since the Gorbals and other places were harbours of vermin and disease, their disappearance is not wholly a cause for regret. But the new housing schemes are unable to contain what was displaced in the old quarters. The demolition of a street damages more than just the buildings which composed it.

★   ★   ★

In Alasdair Gray's novel *Lanark*, the hero Duncan Thaw, an artist, goes out on a sketching expedition with a friend, Kenneth McAlpin. They climb a hill overlooking Cowcaddens on one side and the city centre on the other, and the prospect moves McAlpin to observe that Glasgow is a 'magnificent city', and to ask, 'Why is it that we hardly ever notice that?'

'Because,' replies Duncan Thaw, 'nobody imagines living here . . . Think of Florence, Paris, London, New York. Nobody visiting them for the first time is a stranger because he's already visited them in paintings, novels, history books and films. But if a city hasn't been used by an artist not even the inhabitants live there imaginatively . . .

Imaginatively, Glasgow exists as a music-hall song and a few bad novels. That's all we've given to the world outside. It's all we've given to ourselves.'

If Thaw is right, the cumulative effect on the imagination and sensibility of the people of this dark satanic metropolis over centuries must be monstrous. Gray's own novel is remarkable, not least for providing a major exception to his hero's complaint; it proves that the art of Glasgow fiction is not confined to cheap novels of violence. *Lanark* is actually two novels: one set in the recent past featuring Thaw, a miserably unhappy painter, and the other in an afterworld to which he is consigned after death. Neither section conforms to what Glaswegians have accepted from their literature in the past, and yet in the naturalistic part of the book there is a definite feeling of what it is like to live in this city.

The violent side of Glasgow is a part of the city's culture also, and valuable works have occasionally emerged from that side to sit among Thaw's 'few bad novels' on the shelf. (In particular, *No Mean City*, though not a great literary work and sensationalised in places, is authentic in its rendering of slum life and its values.) This aspect of Glasgow life has, I think, produced an artist whose heroism is equal to Gray's, although he arrived at it by a very different route, and caused a great deal more harm and suffering to himself and others along the way.

When I went to meet Jimmy Boyle properly for the first time (we had met during a brief visit I made for another purpose to Barlinnie Prison two years earlier) I could still visualise the photograph on the front page of the *Evening Times* one Friday night in the mid-1960s. A smirking, baby-faced young man saluted his followers from the steps of the High Court, after walking free from a murder charge for the second time in a year. Within another year, however, they had him in court again, on yet another murder charge, and this time he was locked away for fifteen years.

Now the face was before me: the youthfulness was still there but the smirk had matured into something more appealing and trusting.

He is trim, well mannered and good looking. He beams energy. The only print of many wounds is a long scar on one side of his neck. In parts of the Gorbals, where he comes from, he is a legend and a myth. People stop him in the street and congratulate him for what he has done – not for having been involved in several killings, but for having shown that a man can refuse to be defeated. Boyle spent years in solitary confinement, part of it crouched naked in a narrow cage; he was 'Scotland's most violent man'; triumphantly, he smeared himself in his own excrement to avoid assault, and himself assaulted prison governors and was beaten unconscious in return. He was held in a straitjacket, from which he broke loose, and then a padded cell, from which he also got free. Finally, held to be uncontrollable, he was made the subject of an experiment in penal methods – the Special Unit at Barlinnie Prison in Glasgow, which attempted to tap prisoners' creative resources – and was its first success. His sculpture has been exhibited across the world and been praised by critics ignorant of its origins; he has written a play and an autobiography, *A Sense of Freedom*, which he wrote in prison and then smuggled into the hands of a publisher.

Long before his release, he had begun to devote his energy to a different endeavour and to develop his infamy into a new reputation, but as we spoke his talk was not of his own freedom – but that of his heirs.

'What worries me most when I look around me is the apathy on the streets, among kids especially. Kids are using heroin in a way that's never been known before in Scotland. Fifteen years ago you couldn't get the stuff even if you wanted it – now it's coming in at reduced prices and they're going for it in the way that we used to drink the wine on a Friday night. Why? They look around and what do they see for their future? Nothing. A blank screen, a brick wall. And they're not wrong, are they, because there's not going to be any jobs. The way I see our responsibility is that we've got to tap the creativity that's in people. Otherwise their future – and ours, by the way – is bleak. As someone said to me the other day, apathy is frozen violence.'

Community work was taking up more of his time than sculpture. A block of sandstone had lain untouched outside his front door for months. I had arrived at his house in the morning to find a note attached to the letterbox with my name written on it. It was typed: 'Had to take a young kid in trouble to the social security. If not back by 10 am . . . will be five or ten minutes. Sorry – see you, if you hang around.'

The 'kid', he told me later, was twenty years old, married with two children, and using heroin daily. That morning he had again defeated the patience of his social worker, and, in despair at the possibility of his missing an important interview, she had contacted Jimmy Boyle, who she knew had the boy's confidence. They arrived at the appointed place on time.

Boyle would reject any suggestion that he is 'reformed'. He is, in fact, *trans*formed. His violence was the product of a force he has lately made other use of – metamorphosing violence into art, he has gained a deep understanding of both.

'In the cages I started reading books. I had never read a book in my life until this guy came down the corridor with a trolley and tossed in whatever came to hand. That was it. They gave you one book a week. I used to measure out the pages and divide it up so that I'd have a certain amount to read each day, and I'd keep a little bit extra for Saturday night and give myself a party. Well, the first book I got was *Crime and Punishment* – a popular book inside! – which was a revelation to me, the first revelation. You see, prison forces you to harden yourself to everything around you. I accepted responsibility for what had happened to me, but in the process which I had begun – of trying to pull the place apart – you got pushed more and more and more, and in order to withstand the pressure you had to make yourself harder and harder. And the harder you become, the more painful the process of change is, and for me it was very painful.

'It began properly when the Special Unit was set up. They had tried everything with me and still couldn't contain me. They had tried solitary and that didn't work. They tried the cages and that didn't work. Straitjackets – that didn't work. So what were they going to do? Put me in a cage within a cage within a cage? Instead, they decided to go completely the other way, and started introducing artistic materials into the prison. A woman came along and encouraged us to paint! It was a brave thing to attempt in that coarse world. First of all I did two drawings, portraits, and they were quite good – and I said, Hey! I can do this, I'm good at this! And then I started to do sculpture. I chose sculpture because it's a physical thing and I'm a physical person. I think I was attracted to it because I could get my hands round it, so to speak.

'When I did my first sculpture it was as if – *whoomph!* – a door had opened. A whole new side of myself was suddenly visible, which I was seeing for the first time. I call it a feminine side, which, you see, men in prison can't show. They have to hide it. And that discovery was one of the most exciting moments of my life. I started putting into sculpture certain things expressive of myself which in the past had had nowhere to go – which is a recipe for violence. Sculpture became for me a three-dimensional autobiography in stone. I had covered myself in this hard crust and sculpture blew that crust open. It revealed the female part of me.

'I started working in bronze and then sandstone; I was always searching for a harder material, something with greater permanence. Bronze wasn't hard enough, sandstone wasn't hard enough . . . I really got involved with the personality of different kinds of stones. For example, I had these blocks here brought into the prison from old tenement houses in the Gorbals which were being demolished at the time, and I used them to make these heads, which are actually portraits of characters in a play I'm writing. When I was working on them I would think of all the things that went on behind these walls, of women leaning out of windows gossiping, and so on. I felt that they contained a richness of experience, and it was like I was giving them new life.

'The other prisoners were doing it too. Some of them do what people thought I was doing at first, that's using it as a con. You know, people used to say, "Oh, aye, there's our Jimmy" – wink, wink – "doin' his sculpture" . . . you know, thinking that I was using this as some kind of way of getting time off by being a good boy. And the other prisoners did that and some of them still do. But listen, *they* might think they're conning somebody but *I* know that they're plugged into something which is more powerful than they understand yet; and one day it's going to hit them. One day they'll wake up and find out what it's all about. They'll realise just what they've been playing with – and it'll change them. *That's* what the whole Special Unit's for, not the creation of great works of art, or anything like that. At the end of the day, it comes down to what it does for them. So, even if the prison authorities succeed in undermining the Unit, they'll never destroy the creative spirit which was introduced to it. It's indestructible.'

Boyle the artist has shaped a facet of the Glasgow personality which has been dominant since at least the beginnings of the industrial revolution. That he has done so without recourse either to sentimentality or sensationalism makes his achievement all the more remarkable and unusual. He is one of a very small group of artists – indeed, of human beings – who has seen and known what it is like to be in hell; and he has returned from his experience the bearer of affirmative tidings.

★   ★   ★

It was a blustery day on which to enter September. I spent a night in Drumchapel, one of Europe's largest housing schemes, and then, though Edinburgh called, took a step further west, instead of east, to Clydebank, which shares a boundary with Glasgow.

In the morning I left Drumchapel and its thicker air. Walking down the street I passed a group of girls sitting ten feet up on top of the concrete canopy above the close mouth, one of them wearing her big sister's shoes; below, on the doorstep, three generations of a family looked out over the street or read newspapers; further on, some boys overturned a dustbin and ran off, passing another boy rolling a car tyre in the opposite direction.

Nobody, it seems, would choose to spend a lifetime in Drumchapel or nearby Clydebank, perhaps because – as Duncan Thaw said – nobody has ever imagined living here. And yet people go on living here, in some cases because they have no choice, but in others simply because it has never occurred to them to leave. Their houses have been demolished, members of their families have left, even shipbuilding, the industry which once was Clydebank's *raison d'être*, is no longer the sustaining force it was. The result is that the massive works, not only here but all along the Clyde, once echoing to the sounds of riveters and platers and welders, are now silent, and the skeletons of grand machinery rust in the open air.

The conditions of this town's existence are too fixed to be altered. While there is even a corpuscle of ship oil in the town's bloodstream, it will endure as a separate place. Until I am wiped out completely, it seems to be saying, I cannot begin again.

It seemed, being there, that one's emotions had to be held for the moment in the interstice of a contradiction: for at one and the same time there is the most potent form of life, side by side with that which proposes its negation.

11
Myth Makers

I

A traveller entering Edinburgh in the early eighteenth century, during the final years of the sitting of the Scottish Parliament, would have marvelled at a handsome city in a desolate country. Edinburgh offered the prospect of a great medieval castle perched high upon a rock escarped on both sides, with a loch to the north (it was drained to make way for the New Town, beginning in 1759) and a one-mile-long main street leading eastwards downhill to the former royal residence of Holyrood which, after the removal of the court to London in 1603, became the home of the King's Lord High Commissioner, at that time the Duke of Argyle.

Inside the walls of the city the sights were not so grand. Scotland was poor, and it was poverty which made it difficult for the administrators to withstand proposals for a union with England, which came into effect in 1707. Navigation Acts of 1660 and 1663 had excluded the Scots from trade with English colonies; a scheme to establish a Scottish trading port on the Isthmus of Darien, which connects North and South America, had been a total and very expensive disaster; crop failures in 1695 and three out of the four succeeding years had caused havoc among the rural population, killing perhaps as many as one person in three. In Edinburgh the shops were empty of goods and there were frequent outbreaks of disease – which is not surprising when the general poverty of the nation is considered, together with the unsanitary habits of towns-people of all classes. Until well into the eighteenth century, visitors complained of foul smells in the streets arising from the heaps of excrement lying around. It was necessary to look to one's feet and head at the same time, as the pots were emptied each night from above (upon the given signal of a bell and the cry of 'Gardey loo!') to supplement the piles which already stocked the gutters.

In the houses themselves, master, mistress, family and servants all slept on the floor, in rooms unadorned by pictures on the wall or carpets on the floor: only the largest houses in Edinburgh had carpets, and then only in the most important rooms; and in the smaller towns there might be no carpets at all. The houses rose as high as fourteen storeys, usually with two families on each floor, making twenty-eight large families, of all classes, most with servants (and possibly a French cook), living one on top of the other. 'I believe,' remarked Daniel Defoe, who visited Edinburgh to report on the progress of the Union debates, 'that in no City in the World so many People live in so little Room as at Edinburgh.' He also described the street comprising Lawnmarket, High Street and Canongate as 'perhaps the largest, longest, and finest Street for Buildings and Number of Inhabitants, not in Britain only, but in the World'.

On that street, and in the numerous alleys, wynds and closes running off it, there was no lighting at night, and only the aging members of the Town Guard existed to protect inhabitants and visitors from thieves and pickpockets. Even the most petty crime was met with heavy punishment, and visitors were advised to protect themselves against the utterance of false charges by paying the sum of three guineas to the Kirk Treasurer on entering the city precincts. (Adulterers, however, could not buy protection in this way, and might even be executed.)

The bargain which brought the Union into effect provided for a sum of money to be paid into the Scottish exchequer, partly as compensation for English involvement in the failure of the Darien scheme. The amount was almost exactly what the people of Scotland had raised and lost in that ambitious project: £398,085 10s.

The sum was approved and received by Sir John Clerk of Penicuik, a Baron of the Exchequer, who was solidly in favour of the Union. He was one of those who went south to represent the Scots in the first British Parliament, which accepted sixteen peers (the Scottish Parliament had had 145) and sixty commoners (there had been 160), and he left a record telling how the Scottish Members of

Parliament found themselves 'obscure and unhonoured in the crowd of English society and the unfamiliar intrigues of English politics, where they were despised for their poverty, ridiculed for their speech, sneered at for their manners, and ignored'.

II

It was good to be back – Edinburgh never says 'Welcome' in the voice that Glasgow uses but the expansive gardens off the main street, with the castle behind, speak for themselves – and yet I instantly experienced a sense of fatigue and anti-climax. For weeks I had been looking forward to being here, to seeing familiar faces and old sights, but wouldn't I rather be in Bettyhill? On the steep road between Portmahomack and Rockfield? In the boat between Earraid and Mull? Balhary, Applecross, Rossal . . . Perhaps the chameleon in me was fading at last – and on my own territory! The man who is tired of Edinburgh during the Festival is tired of life? No, but the dressing up, the painted face, the dark rows of seats and the spotlight – the *act* – for once failed to take me in.

But the Festival still suits Edinburgh better than it possibly could any other city in the world, bringing it out of the Scottish sleeping sickness for three weeks of the year, transforming a spectacular ancient monument into a city, with lights, streets which are full at night, pubs busy all afternoon (and all night), and shop windows crammed with posters advertising some of the nine hundred fringe shows.

'What's good this year?' I asked a friend, a playwright, when we met in the pub across the road from my former home. Drinkers spilled from the door on to the pavement, glasses in hand – under normal circumstances an offence in this land of beery over-enthusiasms. From the back came the sound of a guitar and concertina and, a little unusually, a cello being used as a fiddle for the playing of reels.

He spoke of plays so successful that a single performance had sold out the entire run, and of others so bad that after the same night the actors had packed up and left.

'It's a tough business,' he said, raising his glass philosophically. It was, indeed, proving to be tough on him, since a plan to revive one of his plays during the Festival had foundered a month before it started. Two years ago he had won a Festival award for his latest play, and now all he was doing was writing some reviews for a local newspaper.

He looked into his glass, intending to draw attention to its emptiness. I picked it up and walked to the bar. He would have to go, he said, after this one. Festivities had been in progress for over a week, and it was beginning to tell on him. He got out a tin of tobacco and some papers and rolled another cigarette.

Few Scottish writers today are likely to indulge in what Compton Mackenzie and others knew as 'this Scottish business', which usually involved wearing Highland dress and being knowledgeable above all about malt whisky. This one was forty years old, working class, and had begun his university career only after several years out at work. He had not been idle as a writer, but now success and failure were engaged in battle for his future. None of his plays had ever been performed outwith Scotland's boundaries, and the chances of their being published and distributed widely to increase the prospects of future revivals were slender.

'The public in Scotland isn't very interested in drama,' he said. 'They tend to concentrate on drama – if they pay any heed at all – at a very low level. For a start, they want you to have a "name" actor in the play, otherwise the fur-coat-and-pearls brigade won't turn out. And it's very difficult to steer away from the naturalistic convention. Audiences just won't allow it.'

I asked what sort of experiments he had felt hampered in.

'Let me put it this way. It's very difficult to do anything theatrically inventive in Scotland without employing, at some stage, the linguistic medium of Scots. That's my opinion. But then it's very hard to overcome the Scots' own preconceptions about their language. I'm not talking about Gaelic – I mean Scots. It's a strange state of affairs when even in Scotland the use of Scots is taken by audiences as a signal to laugh.

'I used to watch Jimmy Logan at the King's Theatre, and for certain kinds of jokes he would always employ Scots – the jokes were awful but the use of Scots itself was enough to make the audience fall off their

seats with laughter. There's a deeper awareness of Scottish consciousness now than there was then, but a strong Scots tongue still
brings giggles from the stalls. Hardly anyone would have thought of
using Scots for serious dramatic purposes until very recently.'

By 'very recently' I knew he was referring to his own work.

'In England it's exactly the same as it always has been – and so that
means that it stays more or less the same on television too. If you
have a Scot in an English play it's usually because he *is* a Scot, and
they want to use him to portray one of the archaic stereotypes – the
drunk or the hardman or the teuchter with straw coming out his
ears. The same was actually true in Scotland until recently – look
how we perceived ourselves! – but all that nationalistic activity
during the seventies changed things.'

'For good?'

'Oh yes, for good, all right – though the current wave has ended.
There definitely has been a turn in the tide. The failure of the
referendum punctured Scotland and the Scottish identity. And what
you must remember is that it was only the most recent failure. The
Scots are expert at failure. But the tide will turn back again – I'm sure
of that – and I think it will come in far stronger next time.'

I asked if he had ever considered leaving Scotland to go to live in
London. He did not throw up his hands or exclaim with horror at the
suggestion; it was something he had thought about, which he had
calmly reached a decision to reject.

'If I had a play put on at the National Theatre it would benefit me
in two ways: I would start to have more plays performed in England
and I would be able to command a higher quality of actor. But it
wouldn't benefit me artistically, would it? No, my job is to represent
Scotland to the Scots.'

'You would regard yourself as a distinctively Scottish writer?'

'Yes – but also no! No one asks English writers if they are
essentially *English* – it's taken for granted that those questions of
national consciousness are settled by history. But the Scots' history
has done the opposite – so that the Scot, and the Scottish writer in
particular, always has to be asking himself questions about his
national identity, has to be testing himself all the time against his
need for universality. There's this pressure on you in Scotland to be a

recognisably Scottish writer – but it's really much more important just to be getting on with the job. Writers should write – not make patriotic speeches.'

He looked at the clock, drained his glass, stood up and said he must be going. He had to review a play somewhere down in the New Town. I walked part of the way with him, through busy streets, past open doors where actors handed us leaflets advertising their plays, and queues awaited the start of afternoon performances.

Everything was vivacious and ready for creation.

III

'Despised . . . ridiculed . . . sneered at . . . and ignored.' The Scottish inferiority complex; it is at once reassuring and daunting to discover that it has a long and distinguished pedigree.

Scotland – and Edinburgh in particular – copes with present disablement by making the most of the small glories of the past. The capital city's former dignity has gained the force of a myth, but a myth which, instead of strengthening the people's feeling for the present, acts as compensation for it. Except on those rare occasions when the nation functions autonomously – such as at football matches – it is difficult for the Scots to believe in their country as having will and appetites of its own. It is, indeed, forced to feed off the past, an indulgence which has given us Scottish nostalgia, tartanry and Kailyard literature, Sir Harry Lauder, 'a music hall song and a few bad novels'.

'If we do not like the myths we have,' I heard a historian proclaim during a lecture, 'then it is high time we began to construct new ones.' It was a fine sentiment, but the circle is almost closed, for without a political instrument, a nation's will cannot function, and 'new myths', when their creation is attempted, end in the catalogue of failure – and Scotland marches on the spot.

★   ★   ★

The Scottish Nationalists must have thought much on the story of Bruce and the spider, for their own struggle echoes it. A fugitive from Edward I, 'Hammer of the Scots', King Robert the Bruce hid in a cave for weeks on end, and, when his spirits were at their lowest ebb, beheld the spider's persistence in climbing the wall of the cave and took succour from it. Edward died soon afterwards and thereafter Bruce slowly wore down his enemies, ultimately triumphing at the Battle of Bannockburn in 1314.

After a century of official displeasure at the notion of organised patriotic feeling, the 'home rule' movement came to life in the late nineteenth century, slowly gaining momentum until the first major victory in 1945, when Dr Robert McIntyre was elected Scottish Nationalist MP for Motherwell.

It was a freak result which put the first Nationalist in Westminster – the consequence of the Conservatives' inability to run a candidate in a by-election – and it set a pattern which has remained ever since, whereby the SNP benefits from the temporary weakness of one or other of its opponents.

From the start of his career in parliament, McIntyre was regarded as a troublemaker. He began by attempting to draw attention to himself and his cause by refusing to be introduced by a sponsor or to recognise the Mother of Parliaments. He was able to cause only a minor upset among his colleagues, however, for at the general election three months later, with the Conservatives back in action, he was thrown out.

McIntyre is more or less forgotten now and the person in the street, if asked, would be likely to name Winifred Ewing as the first Scottish Nationalist MP. She too won a by-election – in 1967 – and like McIntyre was thrown out at a general election shortly afterwards. But she returned to Parliament later, and by 1974 there were eleven Scottish Nationalists in Westminster, helped on their passage by a strong North Sea wind.

Until the election of Winnie Ewing, the Nationalists were largely regarded by the public as a gaggle of harmless cranks. During the first few days of 1951, for example, the *San Francisco Chronicle* contained a small story about Scotland which described the Scottish Nationalists as 'neither numerous nor important enough to be taken as other than a bit of British humour'. Any Nationalist who read the report, which sneaked into the overseas columns, would naturally have been insulted by it, but the fact that an American newspaper was commenting on the Scottish Nationalists at all was unusual and meant that some one among them had pulled off a stunt which had grabbed the headlines at home.

At the time a leading figure in the movement commented: 'this is the only sort of home rule story that gets a break in the newspapers'. The story in question was the theft of the Stone of Destiny on Christmas Eve 1950, from beneath the Coronation Chair in Westminster Abbey, where it had been since it was removed from Scone Abbey in 1296 in the raids preceding Scotland's successful War of Independence. The superstition of a magic connection between the new monarch and his predecessor when crowned on the stone made it a valuable relic in the middle ages. Over the centuries, promises to return it to Scotland remained unfulfilled, and for some Scots it was a symbol of their nationality, as its continued misappropriation was an act of oppression against them.

The retrieval of the Stone by Ian Hamilton, then a student at Glasgow University, caused a sensation. Together with three fellow conspirators – or 'reivers' as they preferred to be called, after the medieval Border reivers who thrived on raids into England – Hamilton travelled to London with a plan to raid Westminster Abbey while half of London celebrated Christmas and the other half slept it off. They succeeded in stealing the Stone of Destiny and bringing it back home to Scotland.

'It was like the Forty-five all over again,' Hamilton wrote later in his weirdly romantic book, *No Stone Unturned*. 'We might have done something to bring nearer the day when, with great joy and pageantry, the King drove up the Royal Mile to open the Scottish Parliament, while the crowds cheered and the guns of the half-moon battery roared salute.'

The reivers were not members of the Scottish National Party at the time, but of a peculiarly non-political organisation, the Covenant Association, which had broken away from the Scottish National Party following a bout of protracted in-fighting of a sort which has never quite stopped. Its declared goal was self-government for Scotland, but according to an article which appeared in 1951 in its official news-sheet, *New Covenanter*, the covenanters were opposed to 'political action'; self-government', the author of the article stated, 'is not an issue which should be brought into the political arena . . . When a nationalist movement becomes political, passions may be involved which in the long run cannot be controlled, with painful consequences for everyone.'

How characteristically Scottish it sounds. Nationalism without politics. The Scottish Covenant Association issued a further challenge to political logic in its programme by resolving not to fight parliamentary elections. Since violence of any kind was unthinkable, then, progress towards the goal of freedom from English domination could only be advanced by petition or by stunts, such as the theft of the Stone of Destiny, which would strike a symbolic blow for liberty.

'In a few short hours,' Hamilton wrote, 'we planned to show to the English government that there was a limit to their domination of Scotland.'

Four months after the success of the initial adventure, tired of finding new ways of keeping the story in the headlines, the reivers secretly notified the police that the Stone could be found in Arbroath Abbey. It was picked up, promptly returned to Westminster, where the frantic Dean was placated, and the dust settled. The ringleaders in what a supporter called 'one of the most brilliant exploits in Scottish history', reaffirmed their loyalty to the Crown, sold their stories to the Sunday newspapers, and resumed their studies. The reincarnation of Scotland, which the reivers claimed as their goal, fell out of the headlines once again, and history regards it not 'like the Forty-five', but as a stunt.

Once in Edinburgh, I contacted the politician Jim Sillars. Although he had once been a Labour MP, Sillars was now an avowed Scottish Nationalist. Together with another Labour member, he had broken away from the Labour Party in 1975 to form the Scottish Labour Party, which collapsed ignominiously one year later, ejecting Sillars into the Scottish National Party, an organisation he had once said he 'could not stomach'. He lost his seat in Parliament at the next election, but retained a following among the public and the press. One of the country's most perceptive political writers had once predicted the coming of a 'new Scotland . . . and Jim Sillars will surely be one of its leaders'. I wanted to see him not only because of his importance in the political world, but also in connection with his recent appearances in court on a charge of vandalism, arising out of his political activities.

The movement of which he was now a part had made serious advances since Christmas Eve 1950. The climax of one and a quarter centuries of 'Home Rule' campaigning occurred in March 1979, when the referendum to establish the popularity of the proposals to set up a Scottish Assembly in Edinburgh failed to produce the necessary forty per cent vote in favour of the proposals, and the Scotland Bill was defeated. Everything collapsed round about the SNP shortly afterwards, when their force in Westminster was reduced from eleven MPs to two. Emphatically rejected by the voters, the 'Scotland's Oil' campaign an acknowledged flop, the Nationalist movement had to seek new ways of striking blows for Scotland's liberty.

Late in 1981, the SNP made a strange request to the Secretary of State for Scotland, seeking permission to hold a debate on unemployment in the Royal High School building on Edinburgh's Calton Hill, the designated meeting-place of the assembly proposed before the referendum, which was now standing empty. After some deliberation, the request was turned down, setting in motion a train of protest which led to the building being broken into by six SNP members, who intended to occupy it until the day which had been specified for the forbidden debate.

Jim Sillars and two of the others succeeded in gaining entry, but were not inside for long before the police arrived and arrested all six. They had been spotted in the act of entering, and those posted outside had been unable to send a warning, as their radio equipment failed to penetrate the three-foot-thick walls. They were in the Debating Chamber (the school building had been altered in anticipation of housing the assembly) just long enough for Jim Sillars to give a symbolic reading from the Speaker's Chair of 'The Calton Hill Declaration', which had been drawn up specially for the occasion, to the two who had managed to join him inside:

> . . . In taking occupation of this Chamber, we are engaging in a symbolic assertion of Scotland's right to full self-government and the right of the

Scottish people to full employment . . . We call upon the Scottish people to recognise the indivisible link between constitutional change and economic progress and regard this Chamber as an example of how Scottish democracy has been imprisoned by Westminster. We call upon our people to make progress towards an independent sovereign Parliament before the alternative forecast by the working-class martyrs of 1820 becomes a reality: 'Scotland Free or a Desert!'

The six defendants pleaded not guilty to the charge of vandalism (partly because they refused to recognise the description of the premises in the charge as the Royal High School building). While admitting that his method of entry was unorthodox, Sillars claimed that it was a 'reasonable action in this particular case'. The Sheriff disagreed and fined him one hundred pounds, four of the others fifty pounds each, and the case against the sixth was not proven.

However, the 'immense symbolism' of the building to which one of the defendants had alluded in his defence was not diminished by the incident, as witness a small item which appeared in the *Scotsman* a year after the original request to the Secretary of State, whose refusal had precipitated the break-in:

The third of a series of experimental sittings of the Scottish Grand Committee in Edinburgh will take place on Monday, when industry and the economy will be debated by Scottish MPs in the former Royal High School building.

Politics in a nation which is no longer a state is a peculiar business.

I went to the first floor of a handsome New Town building, where the walls were covered in maps of the world and a globe perched on the corner of a bookshelf. Sillars spoke from behind his desk in the same oratorical manner that he used for speeches. He told me that the break-in was part of the campaign of civil disobedience which was launched at the 1981 SNP conference. Its tenets were strictly non-violent but allowed for damage done to property, if deemed necessary to the furtherance of the campaign, and that its ultimate goal was an independent, reincarnated Scotland.

'I don't believe in the United Kingdom. There's no such thing. What we have is England, with appendages. Our campaign of civil disobedience is a calculated risk, with the aim of making the governing of Scotland by Westminster impossible.'

'Do you have any chance of succeeding?'

'Civil disobedience will make Scotland ungovernable within three to four years.'

He looked very sincere when he made this prediction, and I followed my question with another which allowed him to confirm it.

'How do you plan to make the people respond?'

'Look, there's hardly any need for us to do anything. The forces of necessity will do the work for us. If Scotland votes Labour at the next general election and gets another Tory government, then the forces of necessity will drive people to endorse our campaign.'

He described the Calton Hill break-in 'as it might have been', had the SNP leadership not turned its back on the six and disowned their occupation hours before it began.

'We are trying to lay the foundation for change in Scotland. We were trying to do something exciting and adventurous, and look what happened. Had the leadership stuck behind us, then the declaration would have got the publicity it needed and the idea would have spread. Instead, what the public saw was a few reckless individuals denigrated by their political colleagues. What use is that?'

I left the office with the globe on the bookshelf, impressed by his personal magnetism and doubting his chances of success. (Six months later he spun the globe and left the country.) In some ways it was an old story.

'To create the means whereby government becomes unworkable' . . . 'We are committed to an ideal' . . . 'The forces of necessity' . . . It seemed a far cry from Hamilton's typical bit of British humour, his cheering and cap-tossing of over thirty years ago: 'To bring nearer the day when the King drove up the Royal Mile . . . '; 'one of the most brilliant exploits in Scottish history . . . ' But the gulf is only one of vocabulary and of style, for they are actors in the same story, striving to bring a new Scotland into being.

★   ★   ★

Once within Edinburgh city boundaries I knew that the journey was over. Each day brought only a meagre helping of surprises, there was no need to hitch-hike and no more guest houses; the hard beds and dreadful fish suppers and long empty evenings soon seemed like pleasures I would happily embrace again.

I unpacked my maps and waited for the beat of the Festival to draw me in. Instead, I thought of new landscapes.

Walking home along the Royal Mile on the stroke of twelve on the last night of the Festival, as the haar drifted in from the Firth of Forth, I heard a lone piper playing a tune from the Castle ramparts, and once again was momentarily host to the romantic illusion of Scotland. But nothing, not even the self-mocking realisation of the instant's theatricality, could dispel the sense of pure beauty I took home with me.

I returned to the house where I used to live and my friend talked to me of the fantastic meanness of his father, who loathed above all having to give presents. For a silver-wedding anniversary he gave his wife a second-hand copy of *Great Expectations*, with the price – one shilling and sixpence – pencilled in the top right-hand corner of the flyleaf, and underneath in his own hand a scrawled message: 'To my darling wife, for twenty-five years of happiness.'

We spoke, miserably and fearfully, of how the son becomes the father.

Notes

Chapter One

Adelbert Doisy, *The French Prisoners of War in Selkirk*, 1884
Walter Elliot, *The French in Selkirk*, 1982
Graham R. Tomson, *Border Ballads*, 1888

Chapter Three

Charles Tennant, *The Radical Laird*, 1970
William Power, *My Scotland*, 1934

Chapter Six

Alexander Mackenzie, *The History of the Highland Clearances*, 1883
T. C. Smout, *A History of the Scottish People 1560–1830*, 1969
Annie Mackay of Strathnaver's testament of 1886 is quoted in contemporary accounts.
Donald Macleod, *Gloomy Memories*, 1857
The remains of the village of Rossal are now preserved by the Forestry Commission.
John McEwen, *Who Owns Scotland*, 1977. Revised 1981

Chapter Seven

Iain Crichton Smith, *Selected Poems*, 1982
W. F. Skene, *Celtic Scotland*, 1886

Chapter Eight

Who Owns Scotland, revised edition.

Chapter Eleven

Joseph Taylor, *A Journey to Edenborough in 1705*